THE BUMPY ROAD TO BETTER

TIM TIMBERLAKE

THE BUMPY ROAD TO BETTER

UNLOCKING THE HIDDEN POWER IN HARD THINGS

W Publishing Group

An Imprint of Thomas Nelson

The Bumpy Road to Better

Copyright © 2025 Tim Timberlake

All rights reserved. No portion of this book may be reproduced, stored in a retrieval system, or transmitted in any form or by any means—electronic, mechanical, photocopy, recording, scanning, or other—except for brief quotations in critical reviews or articles, without the prior written permission of the publisher.

Published in Nashville, Tennessee, by W Publishing, an imprint of Thomas Nelson.

Thomas Nelson titles may be purchased in bulk for educational, business, fundraising, or sales promotional use. For information, please email SpecialMarkets@ThomasNelson.com.

Scripture quotations marked NLT are from the Holy Bible, New Living Translation. Copyright © 1996, 2004, 2015 by Tyndale House Foundation. Used by permission of Tyndale House Publishers, Carol Stream, Illinois 60188. All rights reserved.

Scripture quotations marked New King James Version are from the New King James Version®. Copyright © 1982 by Thomas Nelson. Used by permission. All rights reserved.

Any internet addresses, phone numbers, or company or product information printed in this book are offered as a resource and are not intended in any way to be or to imply an endorsement by Thomas Nelson, nor does Thomas Nelson vouch for the existence, content, or services of these sites, phone numbers, companies, or products beyond the life of this book.

ISBN 978-1-4003-4604-2 (ePub)

ISBN 978-1-4003-4603-5 (TP)

ISBN 978-1-4003-4605-9 (Audio)

Library of Congress Control Number: 2025932251

Printed in the United States of America

25 26 27 28 29 LBC 5 4 3 2 1

To you—the one who's been through it.

If you're holding The Bumpy Road to Better, *I know life hasn't been easy. Maybe you're still in the thick of it, wondering if better is even possible. If so, hear this: You're not alone.*

This book is for the fighters, the ones who've stumbled but refused to stay down. The road may be rough, but every scar, every tear, every step is shaping something stronger in you.

*So keep going. Keep believing. Better is real.
And I promise—it's worth it.*

*With all my heart,
Tim*

CONTENTS

Introduction: Survival of the Bendiest ix

1. No Thanks, I'm Good 1
   hard asks
2. Everything All at Once 9
   hard balances
3. The Good Fight 17
   hard battles
4. You Have to Start Somewhere 27
   hard beginnings
5. The Power of the Pivot 35
   hard changes
6. Not Your Hill to Die On 45
   hard compromises
7. We Need to Talk 57
   hard confessions
8. Fool Around and Find Out 65
   hard consequences
9. Say What You Need to Say 73
   hard conversations
10. Learning from Donkeys 81
    hard criticism
11. Hold On, Let Me Overthink This 93
    hard decisions
12. The Upside of Downtime 103
    hard delays

13. What Doesn't Kill You Makes You Go to Therapy 113
hard healing

14. Play the Long Game 123
hard losses

15. Time and Chance Happen to Us All 131
hard luck

16. Bridges, Boxes, and Boundaries 141
hard people

17. Ouch.. 151
hard questions

18. It's Not You ... Or Is It? 161
hard rejections

19. You're Not Losing, You're Choosing.................. 171
hard sacrifices

20. This Too Shall Pass 181
hard seasons

21. Wax On, Wax Off 191
hard teachers

22. Eastbound on the South Side of a Mule 201
hard work

Conclusion: You've Got This 211

Acknowledgments 215

Notes 217

About the Author 221

INTRODUCTION

SURVIVAL OF THE BENDIEST

I did some online research recently to discover what animals are the most resilient. I figured cockroaches would be high on the list since they're found everywhere and seem impossible to kill. I was right—they're horrifyingly tough. But another creature I had never heard of turned out to be even more resilient than cockroaches. It's called a *tardigrade*, also known as a water bear or moss piglet. If you've never heard of tardigrades, google them. Go ahead; I'll wait.

Tardigrades are microscopic creatures that live in water and damp environments, and they are either adorable or terrifying, depending on which picture you look at. Despite their miniscule size, they are ridiculously adaptable, hardy, and tenacious little guys. They can last thirty years without food or water, endure temperatures from near absolute zero (-460°F) to above boiling, withstand pressure up to six times greater than the deepest point of the ocean, survive in the vacuum of space, and resist radiation.[1] They are invisible to the naked eye, yet they survive and thrive under circumstances that would crush, freeze, burn, starve, or vaporize most living things. And they look good doing it.

You'll likely never face physical conditions anywhere close to those extremes. But you *will* face difficult situations in life. I'm sure you already have. You might even be going through some hard things right now. Whether the struggle is physical, mental, emotional, or relational, you need to know how to survive and thrive under pressure.

In other words, like water bears, we need *resilience* to recover quickly from difficulties and adapt to challenging circumstances with strength and perseverance. Resilience helps us survive and thrive in hard times. It allows us to withstand pressure, pivot as needed, and find a way forward. It enables us to bend rather than break.

Here's what I want you to know, though: Many of the hard things we experience in life are not just inevitable—they are essential. They are good for us in some way. Maybe they teach us, or they shape us, or they purify us, or they move us forward. The difficult is temporary, but the reward we receive on the other side of those things is permanent.

The problem is that we'll often do just about anything to avoid hard things. We choose easy jobs rather than embracing hard work. We get our feelings hurt by hard criticism, so we don't listen to people who could help us. We avoid hard battles, even though freedom waits on the other side. We cancel people rather than having hard conversations with them, thereby ruining relationships. And the list goes on. Our pursuit of comfort can keep us from achieving our dreams and fulfilling our potential.

The Bumpy Road to Better is about developing resilience so you can go *through* the difficult situations that will make you better rather than avoiding them or being crushed by them. We're going to explore twenty-two different "hard things" that every one of us faces in life. In each, the goal is to discover not only how to stay strong under pressure but how to make the most of each opportunity.

It's a bumpy road, but the bumps are only making you better. They're forming your adaptability, building your faith, sparking your creativity, jump-starting your courage.

Most important, you aren't doing this alone. God isn't surprised by the hard things you face, and he doesn't abandon you when you need him most. He's right there with you, helping you make the most of every moment. It's so important to participate in the process, though. On the bumpy road to better, you choose whether hard moments build you or break you, shape you or shatter you, purify you or paralyze you.

You are built to survive and thrive under even the most challenging of circumstances, as strong and resilient as the tardigrade. And hopefully you'll even look good while doing it.

CHAPTER 1

NO THANKS, I'M GOOD

(Hard Asks)

I had LASIK surgery on my eyes more than ten years ago, and it wasn't exactly what I imagined it would be. The result was great, but the recovery process was *miserable*.

I had astigmatism, so my corneas were shaped like footballs rather than basketballs. That was the doctor's metaphor because he knows I am a sports guy. On a practical level, this meant the surgery was a lot more invasive than I expected, and the recovery was a lot harder. The pain was terrible and made worse by light, so for several days I wore patches on both eyes, like a pirate with really bad luck.

For someone who likes to be in constant motion, that was frustrating. I needed help with countless things I was used to doing by myself. I had to depend on Jen, my wife, to guide me around the house and find the bathroom. I even had to trust her when she drove, which can be terrifying when you can't see where you're going.

Jen has dealt with a lot of chronic pain in her life, so I was used to helping her with *her* pain. Now I had to ask her to make me coffee, bring me food, drive me to the doctor, and read my text messages. She was by my side, assisting me with whatever I needed. That was surprisingly hard for me to handle.

I learned something about myself during that time: I have a difficult time asking for help. I don't know why. Maybe it hurts my pride.

Maybe I don't like to bother people. Maybe I don't want to be seen as weak. Maybe I like to be in control. Probably all those things are true, along with a few others.

This is what I mean by "hard asks." There is something built into me—and possibly into you—that resists asking others for help. But if we can't handle the discomfort of requesting needed assistance, if we can't push past the awkwardness, embarrassment, and vulnerability of saying "I need you," we're going to miss out on the things only other people can provide.

We All Need Help Sometimes

Is it hard for you to ask for what you need? Do you seek advice when you're facing a tough decision, or do you just take your best guess? Do you ask for directions when you're lost, or do you drive in circles and curse Google Maps? Do you ask for assistance locating the tomato sauce in the grocery store, or do you wander the aisles for twenty minutes, mumbling under your breath? Do you read instruction manuals when you assemble IKEA furniture, or do you figure it out as you go, only to end up with seven extra screws that will surely come back to haunt you? When someone offers to help you, do you say, "No thanks, I'm good," when you're clearly not?

I'm not criticizing you for being independent. I'm the same way, as I already mentioned, and I think there's a lot to be said for developing the independence, creativity, and stick-to-itiveness you need to figure things out on your own. But that's not always the right option.

Sometimes you need help, and that's okay.

God knows this. Once he finished creating the world, his first act was to design a teammate for Adam: Eve. God said, "It is not good for the man to be alone. I will make a helper suitable for him" (Genesis 2:18). The term *helper* here isn't about hierarchy, as if God were saying, "Adam, you need an assistant you can boss around." It's actually a word used to describe God himself at times. He was saying, "Adam, don't try to do this alone. That will not end well. You need someone you can lean on and learn from; someone you can work with and walk beside."

Ecclesiastes 4:9–12 makes it clear that we need other people:

> Two are better than one,
> because they have a good return for their labor:
> If either of them falls down,
> one can help the other up.
> But pity anyone who falls
> and has no one to help them up.
> Also, if two lie down together, they will keep warm.
> But how can one keep warm alone?
> Though one may be overpowered,
> two can defend themselves.
> A cord of three strands is not quickly broken.

If you think a request for aid is a sign of weakness, you're going to limit yourself. That's a self-inflicted wound, my friend. There are people in your world who would be happy to give you what you need—a hand, a loan, a word of advice, or a swift kick in the pants, as my dad used to say—so why would you try to be the Lone Ranger?

Take your finances, for example. There's no shame in recognizing that you might not have the greatest spending habits, or that you never learned how to budget, or that nobody in your family showed you how to save for retirement. The only shame would be in not seeking the knowledge you need to move forward in a more financially responsible way.

Or consider your love life (or lack thereof). If you are having issues with your significant other, you don't have to choose between constant fighting or calling it quits. There are other options, but they start with admitting that what you're doing now isn't working and you need help.

How about your career? Is there anything you need that is on the other side of a hard ask? Should you ask for a raise? Ask to be mentored? Ask to lead a project? Ask to be moved to another department? Ask how you could improve? Ask what classes or certifications you should add to your résumé? Ask for recommendations? Ask for a job?

Finances, relationships, and careers are just three out of dozens of areas where you might need to swallow your pride, silence your fear, and seek help. Ask yourself: *What do I need right now? What would make my life better? What would help me overcome the obstacles that are holding me back? What do I need that someone else has and might be willing to share?*

List three or four things you could reasonably request from people in your world. Then ask yourself these important questions: *Why is this such a hard ask for me? Why do I hesitate to ask for help?*

Why Don't We Ask for Help?

Remember, resilience refers to your capacity to endure, adapt to, and bounce back from hard things. "Hard asks" are about building resilience to whatever obstacles keep you from asking for help. In other words, *I want you to get used to depending on other people.*

What might be stopping you from asking for help? Here are a few possibilities.

1. You don't know what you don't know.

Maybe you don't realize you need help. You don't know what you don't know, after all. So you keep making the same mistakes or butting up against the same wall, not realizing help is available if you'd just ask. That feeling of frustration is meant to be a red flag alerting you to a need for change. What questions have you never thought to ask?

2. You've always done things on your own.

Maybe you never learned how to ask for help. You've always done things on your own, so seeking assistance feels foreign to you. You might blame that on your personality, but what if it's just the force of habit and you need to create new habits of interdependence, humility, and community?

3. You think it's not okay not to be okay.

Maybe you've been taught that weaknesses should be hidden. You know you're not enough, but asking for aid would be too vulnerable. It would mean exposing your ignorance, lack of experience, mistakes, or limitations. So you choose to suffer in silence behind the façade of "No thanks, I'm good!" If you don't give yourself permission not to be okay, you won't get the help you need to be okay.

4. You're embarrassed to admit you need help.

Maybe you don't want to admit someone else has something you don't: a talent, a resource, a character quality, a connection. Asking for help is vulnerable. It feels humiliating, so you'd rather avoid it. But pride is a liar, and ego is an enemy. It's hard to humble yourself, but the reward of humility is the help you urgently need.

5. You like to be in control.

First of all, control is an illusion. None of us are "in control" of everything all the time. Asking for something doesn't mean you are giving someone else power over you. You can ask for what you need without losing yourself or selling out. In reality, asking is part of autonomy because you choose when to ask and when not to. You're still in control, but in a good way.

I invite you to take a closer look at your own life by reading through this list again and being brutally honest with yourself. Think about different challenges or frustrations you're experiencing. Is it hard for you to ask for help in any of those areas? And if so, why? What does your silence reveal about areas for potential growth?

Getting H.E.L.P.

Identifying the *reasons* you don't ask for help is the first step toward making real change. The second step is *asking* for help. Once you've dealt with any inner issues that are keeping you from seeking assistance, it's time to make yourself vulnerable and reach out for help. The following acronym breaks down four practical steps to begin asking for what you need.

H: Humble yourself

As I mentioned earlier, this is difficult for most of us, but it's a necessary step, and it brings freedom. We often want to "fake it till we make it" but aren't even close to making it, and we need to quit faking it and get some advice, training, or aid.

Appearing to have it all together is overrated. It's much better to develop a mindset of humility, one always open to change and growth. Proverbs 9:9 says, "Instruct the wise and they will be wiser still; teach the righteous and they will add to their learning." You'll never outgrow the need to be humbly curious.

E: Explain your need clearly

In order to be clear in your communication, you'll need to be clear in your own mind. Take time to analyze your situation and determine what you need. Too often we feel frustrated, angry, or overwhelmed, but we don't move past the emotion and determine objectively what we need to move forward.

Another note here: Don't sit around feeling sorry for yourself and wishing someone would offer to help. Take the initiative to reach out and ask for what you need. Sure, someone might say no. But that's better than never asking in the first place. If you ask enough people—and the right people—you can nearly always find the answers, advice, or aid you need.

L: Let other people in

This is one of the hardest parts about asking for help, but it's also one of the best. Receiving help from others means allowing them to have some level of input and influence in your life. You don't have to give them complete access, but you do need to lower your defenses, open your heart, and expand your world. Remember, you weren't designed by God to do life alone. Let other people in. You need them, and they need you. There's no shame in leaning on others. There's strength in it.

P: Plan your next step

The final step is to act based on the help you've received. This is where the rubber meets the road and you must make changes that move you forward. If you've identified your need, asked for help, and received help, make the most of it. You've been given a gift; now you're responsible to use it.

While it's good to *lean* on people at times, it's not good to *leech* from people all the time. There's a big difference. Having a plan of action ensures that you use people's help as a springboard for advancement rather than becoming dependent on them in unhealthy ways.

This step will also reveal if you truly want to move forward or not. It's easy to blame a lack of resources when you're struggling with something such as your finances, an addiction, or some other challenge, but there might be some inner obstacles as well. When you get help from others, meet their sacrifice with your own courage and commitment. Let this be the moment you break free from past habits or mental models and step into the bigger future God is calling you to.

Whom do you need to ask for help? For advice? For a job? For training? For feedback? For forgiveness? Or even . . . for a date?

Don't let barriers have the last word. You can do this. You can ask for what you want, and on the other side of the hard ask, you'll find the answers and aid you need.

Hard Asks: Questions for Reflection

1. When was a time you struggled to ask for something you needed, but you overcame the resistance and asked for it? What did you learn in the process?
2. Do you tend to quickly seek help when you need it, or is that more of a last resort? Which of the five reasons for not seeking help resonated with you the most?
3. What is an area of frustration you are dealing with? Whom could you reach out to for assistance? What would you ask for specifically? How do you think they would respond?

GETTING BETTER THROUGH BUMPS

Write down a specific "hard ask" you've been avoiding or resenting. What are the consequences of not addressing this? What are the benefits of addressing it? What practical step will you take *today* to embrace this hard ask?

CHAPTER 2

EVERYTHING ALL AT ONCE

(Hard Balances)

I remember sitting in eighth-grade economics class and watching the teacher set an empty glass jar on his desk. He proceeded to fill it with large rocks, all the way to the brim. Then he asked the class, "Is this jar full?"

We all said yes. The teacher pulled out a bag of smaller rocks and started dropping them in, and he kept shaking the jar until the smaller rocks had filled in the empty spaces around the big rocks. He asked again, "Is this jar full now?"

It looked full, but by then we had figured out it might be a trick question, so there were fewer yeses. Next he took out a bag of sand and poured the contents in until the sand reached the top. Again he asked us, "Is the jar full now?"

Nobody said yes. We watched as he brought out a pitcher of water and poured the contents into the jar. We couldn't believe how much water fit into something that appeared to be so full.

Then he asked us one more question: What would have happened had he started with the sand and little rocks? Obviously the largest rocks would not have fit.

To be honest, I don't remember what point he was making about economics. The illustration stuck with me, though. It reminds me that *the order of things matters*. My teacher didn't have to choose between the large rocks and the small rocks, but he did have to choose their order.

The same holds true in life. What you do first determines what you can do next. Sometimes we feel like we must choose between two things when in reality we need to get better at choosing the order we do them in. If we can get the order right, we'll be able to fit a lot more into our budgets, schedules, and minds.

On the other hand, if we don't pay attention to the order of things, we'll always feel like there's not enough of us to go around.

Not enough time.

Not enough energy.

Not enough money.

Not enough focus.

Not enough _____.

I've been there before, and I'm sure you have too. We think life is too much and we are too little. We keep trying to do everything all at once, and it leaves us overwhelmed.

The bad news is that life isn't going to get any simpler. So instead of complaining about how complicated things are and wishing we could move to the beach and get away from it all, we need to develop better resilience. That doesn't mean gritting our teeth and trying harder—it means adapting and growing so we can handle more pressure with less panic.

The good news is that "hard balances" aren't about doing everything perfectly all at once. That's not balance. That's chaos waiting to happen. Nobody can keep that up for long.

Nor is balance about giving everything the same weight—the same attention, time, or investment. That doesn't work for me, and I don't think it works for anyone. We can't treat everything like the large rocks in my illustration. Sure, everything we're doing matters, but not every part matters equally.

Rather, balance means *the entire system of our lives* should work together in a coordinated, structured, intentional way. That's why balance begins with setting our priorities in order.

Priorities Lead to Balance

True balance happens by choosing the rocks that go first, then the ones that go second, then the sand and water that go next. Getting the order right produces a calmer, more focused life. It puts our calendar, relationships, and goals into greater perspective. It restores balance.

In the Bible, we find numerous reminders to pay attention to the order of things. One of the most famous is found in Matthew 6:33–34, when Jesus said: "But seek first his kingdom and his righteousness, and all these things will be given to you as well. Therefore do not worry about tomorrow, for tomorrow will worry about itself. Each day has enough trouble of its own." Jesus reminded us that priority number one is God. Getting that right will help the rest fall into place.

Another example is found in Proverbs 24:27, which is focused on work and financial priorities: "Put your outdoor work in order and get your fields ready; after that, build your house."

In every arena of life, if you keep first things first, you'll be able to figure out the rest much more easily. Balance starts with getting your priorities in order.

- What do you think about first each day?
- What goes into your schedule first and doesn't move easily?
- What do you finish first when multiple things compete for your attention?
- What do you give the first of your time and energy to?
- What do you spend money on first when you have extra income?
- What do you talk about first when you're in conversation with others?

Questions such as these help you understand what truly matters so you can fit the things you need to do or want to do into your schedule. If you don't consider these questions, some of those things will get squeezed out by the hustle and grind of life. This focus on intentionality and wise living was the heart behind my book *The Power of 1440*. My father passed away when I was a young man, and I learned early on that every day is a gift. We are called by God to make the most of each moment. While it's tempting to assume that if you just work harder or organize better you'll suddenly be enough for it all, the truth is that life will often be "too much." Instead of working harder on everything, work first on what matters most.

Defining your priorities is a way of saying, "These are the big rocks in my jar. These are my nonnegotiables. These have to go in first, and I'll arrange everything else around them." This brings balance by helping us put each area in proper relationship to the rest. My job doesn't get the same weight as my family. My family doesn't get the same weight as God. My desires don't get the same weight as my purpose. My job doesn't get the same weight as my peace.

What are the "large rocks" in your life? Have you written them down? Are you making sure to plan for those first, then fit the smaller things into the gaps around them?

This is up to you. We're talking about your life, your future, your values, your goals. What will you prioritize? What will you cancel? What will you postpone? What will you delegate? What will you do today? What will you focus on right now?

This goes beyond being an *organized* person—at least in the way we usually use the word: having everything neat, orderly, planned, and controlled. That works for some personality types, but a lot of people would go crazy in that kind of setting.

What I'm talking about here is an internal order of priorities. While this will help give order to your day, it doesn't mean your day will look how someone else expects it to. As a matter of fact, having your priorities in order might mean putting down the phone or shutting the laptop when your kids want to play, even though your never-ending workload will suffer a little.

Rather than letting your life be run by the tyranny of the urgent, figure out what matters the most to you and keep that front and center. Then find creative ways to fit in the other priorities as well. You'll be surprised how effective and efficient you can be when you set priorities and learn to create balance.

The Pace of Peace

So how do we know what to spend our time and energy on? While this is an individual choice (meaning you have to decide for yourself), I can tell you one thing that has helped me greatly over the years: the peace of God. I call this moving at the pace of peace.

If something is God-ordained, it will come with peace. There will be an inner sense of God's leading, God's pleasure, God's will.

The opposite is also true. If something is not God-ordained, your peace will evaporate. Things might seem great on the outside, but you'll know something is missing on the inside. I determined a long time ago that if it costs me my peace, it's too expensive.

Of course, peace and comfort are not the same thing. You can be uncomfortable and still have peace. You can work really hard and still have peace. You can walk through the valley of the shadow of death and still have peace. You can be confused, alone, scared, or in pain and still have peace. You can wish you were doing just about anything else and still have peace.

Sometimes you have peace at the beginning, and it guides your steps. Other times you take steps to the best of your ability, and peace follows. Don't be too quick to reject things just because they aren't what you expected or they seem too difficult. If God is in it, you'll experience his peace.

My wife and I got married the fifth time we saw each other in person. That's a story for another chapter, but the reason we were able to take such a significant step was because we both felt a deep, uncommon peace. We knew our relationship was from God, and we let his peace lead us. We've never regretted that decision.

The peace of God allows you to enjoy the season you are experiencing and the activity you are engaged in today. As Jesus said, "Tomorrow will worry about itself" (Matthew 6:34). Learn to follow the pace of God's peace, regardless of where it leads.

There's a famous passage in Ecclesiastes that says:

> There is a time for everything,
> and a season for every activity under the heavens:
> a time to be born and a time to die,
> a time to plant and a time to uproot,
> a time to kill and a time to heal,
> a time to tear down and a time to build,
> a time to weep and a time to laugh,
> a time to mourn and a time to dance.
> (3:1–4)

The passage goes on for several more verses. The point is that everything has its time—but that time is not necessarily now. So be patient. Be wise. Keep your priorities straight. Enjoy the moment. And most of all, move at the pace of peace. It's not as loud as other voices that might be hollering your name—the voices of debt or fear or the demands of others or temptation—but it's far more trustworthy.

Shift the Weight

Besides getting your priorities in order and moving at the pace of peace, there is another key to maintaining balance: shifting your weight.

When I was seven, my dad tried to teach me to wrestle. He was a big guy: six feet, five inches, and 270 pounds. I was a little shrimp, a string bean, probably fifty pounds soaking wet. I remember asking him how I could possibly move him since I wasn't strong enough to lift him.

He told me the only way to move something you can't lift is to use its own weight. When he would come at me, he showed me how to pull him closer and utilize his weight as momentum, then direct the weight where I wanted it to go. If I could keep *my* balance while getting him off *his* balance, I could beat him (or at least not lose as badly).

I've often thought of that in relation to the weight of life. The thing about balance is that you don't realize you have it until you lose it. And by then, it's often too late. We have to learn to keep our balance while shifting the things that come toward us onto the Lord. That's what "Cast all your anxiety on him because he cares for you" means (1 Peter 5:7). It's a weight shift.

You can't cast your cares and carry them at the same time. It's one or the other. Too many of us think we're casting our weight on God, but we still carry it, or attempt to, anyway.

My dad often told me that if your opponent takes down your head, your body will follow. The head is the highest point, and it affects your center of gravity. You have to prioritize your head or you'll throw off your entire balance.

The real fight is going on inside your head. It's your thoughts, your mindset, your attitude, your perspective. If you're struggling to find balance, prioritize your head. Protect your thoughts. Cast your anxieties on God so you have a clear head and heart. The attacks won't last forever, but they come hard and fast, and you have to stay levelheaded.

These three keys—order your priorities, move at the pace of peace, and shift the weight—take effort and intentionality, but they are absolutely doable. And they are within your power today.

Don't settle for a life of constantly feeling like you're not enough. Don't let *overwhelmed* be the adjective that describes how you show up in the world. Instead, build a balanced, simple life that relies on God and enjoys every season.

Hard Balances: Questions for Reflection

1. What areas of your life feel out of balance right now? How could prioritizing the "large rocks" help bring things into better alignment?
2. What does it mean to "move at the pace of peace"? Think of a time when you clearly sensed God's peace (or a lack of peace) in a decision or season of life. How did you respond?
3. What does it mean to "shift the weight"? What burdens are you carrying right now that you need to cast on God? What would that look like practically?

Getting Better Through Bumps

Write down a specific "hard balance" decision you've been avoiding or resenting. What are the consequences of not addressing this? What are the benefits of addressing it? What practical step will you take *today* to pursue a hard balance?

CHAPTER 3

THE GOOD FIGHT

(Hard Battles)

When my son, Max, was five years old, we went to Disney World in Orlando as a family. Max told us before we got there that his favorite ride was Slinky Dog. He kept saying, "I'm gonna go on the Slinky Dog ride all day. I'm gonna ride it ten times in a row."

The only problem was he had never been on the Slinky Dog ride. He had just seen advertisements for it, and he had always been a big fan of Slinky from the *Toy Story* movies. When we got to the park and he saw the thing in real life, he panicked. He said it was too big, too fast, and too loud.

I told him, "Hey man, you have to ride this. This is what you wanted. You'll love it."

Max refused. He came up with a whole storyline about why he couldn't ride it: He was sick, he had to use the restroom, and so on.

I could tell he wanted to ride it but was too scared, so I pushed a little harder. "No, Max, we're going to ride it. You've got this."

He wasn't fully convinced, but he stayed in line. He fought with fear and he won. He went on that ride like a champ, and when he got off, he turned to me and said, "I told you I could do it, Dad!" From then on, Slinky Dog was his favorite ride—not because he imagined it but because he experienced it.

Max had to fight a battle. It was a battle of fear and insecurity.

While his struggle might seem small to an adult, to a five-year-old, it was the biggest fight he'd ever faced. He won that fight, and it propelled him forward.

Life is like that for all of us. We face countless enemies: fear, temptation, anxiety, abuse, trauma, addiction, pride, greed, loneliness, financial troubles, physical illness, and so much more. No sooner do we win one fight than another shows up to take its place. Some battles are big, while others are little. Some are painful and difficult, while others are relatively easy. Some are over quickly, and others drag on for what feels like forever.

You're going to face battles as long as you live, which means you need to get better and better at fighting them and winning them. Remember, the answer to hard things—including hard battles—isn't to run away from them. It's to develop greater resilience, which means figuring out how to respond and react in wiser ways.

Toward the end of his life, Paul told Timothy, "I have fought the good fight, I have finished the race, I have kept the faith" (2 Timothy 4:7). I love that description: the good fight. Paul didn't run from battles, even when they were hard and his very life was on the line. He didn't resent the opposition or get an attitude about the challenges. He simply kept going, kept showing up, kept fighting. It was a hard fight, but it was a good fight, a necessary fight, a productive fight.

You might be going through a hard battle right now, maybe more than one. Please know that you're fighting the good fight. God is proud of you, and he's standing next to you saying, "You've got this!" While the battle might feel overwhelming and fear is shouting in your ear right now, I believe you'll be on the other side of the fight soon, and you're going to feel the thrill of victory.

Mortal Enemies Are Mere Mortals

In the good fight of faith, you must constantly remind yourself of this foundational truth: You are not alone. Your heavenly Father is by your side, and he believes in you more than anyone. When David was facing the possibility of death at the hands of his enemies, he wrote:

> When I am afraid, I put my trust in you.
> In God, whose word I praise—
> in God I trust and am not afraid.
> What can mere mortals do to me?
> (Psalm 56:3–4)

Note David didn't deny his fear. He said, "When I am afraid," which means this was a regular occurrence. He simply used fear to point him to the God in whom he trusted, his ever-present source of help. He knew the power of his enemies, and he felt genuine, valid fear. But he also knew it could not compare to the power of his God. When he remembered that, he became unafraid.

Who are the "mere mortals" that threaten you today? Can you see beyond their intimidating size and power and recognize that the God who is with you and for you is far greater than any enemy you face on this planet? They might be terrifying, but in comparison to God, they are merely human.

This doesn't refer just to people. It refers to any human experience. Maybe you are struggling with debt. That's a battle. It's hard to stay faith-filled when the bills are piling up. It's difficult to hold on to your integrity when things are desperate. But you have to keep believing for financial stability and God's blessing. He is bigger than debt. He is not intimidated by lack. He is not limited by human economies or recessions or bankruptcy or job markets. Your mortal enemies are merely mortal, while the God you serve is sovereign over the universe.

Maybe you're dealing with a family conflict. That's a battle too. It's an ongoing challenge to keep forgiving, to keep reaching out, to keep believing the best. Don't fight alone, though. God created family.

He designed love. He put the desire for family within you, and he gives you the capacity and creativity you need to fight for reconciliation.

When you feel afraid because of the obstacles and enemies that threaten you, do what David did. Put your trust in God. Remind yourself that the God you serve created the universe. He is infinitely bigger than anything this human world can throw at you.

The Secret to Winning Hard Battles

It's human nature to want quick fixes and guaranteed solutions. We love books with titles like *Ten Foolproof Ways to Get Whatever You Want Right Now* or *How to Fix Everything Without Actually Doing Anything*. Books like these sell easy answers, but easy answers don't win hard battles.

You know what does? Perseverance. Sticking it out. Staying in line at Slinky Dog with brave tears running down your face because you know that what's on the other side of this battle is worth the fight.

Every battle is different. Every challenge has layers and levels. I don't think anyone else can fully define what "winning" means in your particular situation, which makes it impossible for me to give you a step-by-step, foolproof strategy to win your battle. But I can tell you this: If you don't give up, God himself will show you how to win it.

Stay in the fight. That's the secret to winning. Keep showing up, keep trying, keep believing, keep fighting. If you focus on how you engage today, the winning will take care of itself.

That might look like getting out of bed in the morning, even when depression is trying to drain your will to move. It might mean sending a text message to an estranged family member, seeking reconciliation for the twentieth time. It might involve choosing to work another ten-hour day, even though you've been building your business for two years and it still hasn't taken off.

Battles don't last forever. They feel eternal while you're fighting them, but they have an end date. When the battle is over and the dust settles, will you still be here? That's what matters most. And I promise you: The taste of victory lasts longer than the pain of the struggle.

You'll make mistakes during the fight. You'll get wounded from time to time. You'll lose some things along the way, and that's never easy. But if you can stick it out till the end, you'll win. Perfection isn't the goal here; perseverance is.

Perseverance is so important because even when our problems are external, such as money or health or relational issues, our biggest battle is always internal. Paul wrote, "For our struggle is not against flesh and blood" but rather against spiritual opposition (Ephesians 6:12). Our real enemies are fear, greed, pride, and a host of other mindsets and emotions that try to take us out.

Don't get so caught up in the external fight that you neglect the internal one. In desperate times it's all too easy to focus on what you should *do*, but how you should *think* is far more important. That's why you have to protect your head, as we saw earlier. You won't stay in the fight if you don't think you can win it. But if you can triumph on the inside by keeping your trust in God and your eyes on the victory ahead, you'll triumph on the outside too. It's just a matter of time.

God Gives You Plot Armor

If you want to win internally so you can win externally, you need to see a bigger picture than just the struggle at hand. Don't let the heat of the battle rob you of perspective. This is a chapter in your life, but it's not the whole story. And it's moving you forward.

In movies and storytelling, main characters often have something called "plot armor." It's a term used to describe someone who is safe from harm no matter what happens because they are essential to the plot. I'm sure you've seen movies like this. The hero can be in the most intense battle scene ever, but somehow he survives. He can fall off cliffs, get in car wrecks, or be thrown into a rock wall by a fantastical creature, and he just shakes it off and keeps fighting.

In a very real sense, you and I have plot armor. It's God's plot armor because he is the storyteller. We're main characters. We're essential to the plot, and he holds our lives and futures in his hand. Even when things don't work out the way we expect, we can rest in the knowledge that God's master plan cannot be frustrated, shaken, or thwarted. Remember, too, that his care for us extends beyond this life, which means that our current struggles should be seen in the light of eternity. We matter deeply to him, and as the days and years go by, our story will always unfold under his watchful eye and careful hand.

"Plot armor" doesn't mean you can do stupid things without consequences, of course. Life isn't a Marvel movie. The danger is real, and you have to be cautious, wise, and alert. But even when you're in danger, you're safe with God. You are fighting from a place of security because you know God is with you. I love how Psalm 91 describes our security in God.

> You will not fear the terror of night,
> nor the arrow that flies by day,
> nor the pestilence that stalks in the darkness,
> nor the plague that destroys at midday.
> A thousand may fall at your side,
> ten thousand at your right hand,
> but it will not come near you.
> (vv. 5–7)

Have faith in a God who keeps you safe, a God who already knows how he will deliver you, a God who sees the whole story at once. Keep your eyes on the bigger picture. There is life beyond this battle, and you need to be ready to move forward once it is over.

Winning Doesn't Always Feel Like It

You can have divine plot armor and still lose some things along the way. You need to understand this because in order to win, you often have to give up a few things, and the pain of loss can make it *feel* like you're losing, even when you're winning. (On the flip side, the pleasures this world has to offer can make you feel like you're winning even when you're losing—but that's a truth for another chapter.)

Consider the final hours of Jesus' life, hanging on a cross between two criminals. His disciples and friends had abandoned him. The crowds he had healed and fed now mocked and reviled him. The religious leaders who should have protected him had orchestrated his execution. Worst of all, the God he served had forsaken him—or at least it felt that way.

In the eyes of everyone, he was losing.

But in reality, it was the greatest victory this broken world has ever seen.

The losses you and I face are smaller than that, but the principle is the same. Sometimes in the middle of the battle it can feel like you're losing, even when you're really winning. You are making progress. You are learning. You are growing. You are changing. You are becoming the person God designed you to be.

You might feel like you're losing, but don't judge too quickly. You might be on the verge of your greatest victory.

Yes, there is a price. Greatness is going to cost you. It will make you uncomfortable, cause inconvenience, and bring you pain. If you aren't willing to pay the price of greatness, you'll never achieve it.

Often, we discover these costs in the heat of the battle. Battles point out the things that are holding us back and slowing us down. They sharpen our senses, increase our self-awareness, build resilience, and challenge our mindsets. *Battles build us.* But the building happens only if we're willing to accept the sacrifices our battles demand. This is where resilience comes in, because we need to develop our capacity to sustain losses without losing our courage or stability.

Sometimes I ask myself, *What am I willing to sacrifice or walk away from so my life can be advanced and I can be stronger? What will I lose so that I can gain? What do I need to leave behind, change, or learn today?*

I know athletes who wake up at four in the morning in the off-season to train so that when the sports season begins, it feels easier than training did. I know many who don't drink, who don't go to clubs, who don't stay out all night, because they'd rather set aside some privilege and pleasure in order to win their battle for greatness. They understand they are in a battle for their own future, and certain things must be left behind.

It's the power of no. To win battles, you often have to stop doing some things you like doing. But what you say no to determines what you can say yes to.

Author and researcher Jim Collins famously wrote, "Good is the enemy of great. And that is one of the key reasons why we have so little that becomes great.... Few people attain great lives, in large part because it is just so easy to settle for a good life."[1]

What battles are you fighting? What price are you paying? Are you willing to do what it takes to win that battle, even if it comes with a cost? For example, are you willing to make a "hard ask" and request assistance from someone else? Are you fighting the right battle, or do you need to face the "hard balance" question of priorities? The premise of this book is that *better* lies on the other side of *bumpy*, and often it's this bumpiness, this price we must pay, that separates winning battles from losing them.

Notice that the sacrifices you are called to make aren't necessarily "sinful" things, but they are keeping you from greater things ahead, and they're not supposed to go with you into the next battle. Maybe it's offense or bitterness you need to leave behind. Maybe it's a bad habit. Maybe it's a hobby that takes too much of your time. Maybe it's a mindset that is handcuffing you to your current situation. Maybe it's your pride or your comfort.

Whenever God reveals something that is holding you back in the battle, remember this: That thing is not worth holding on to. Let it go; set it down; leave it behind. God has greater things in store.

The challenges you're facing and the battles you're fighting are certainly bigger than Slinky Dog. But the principle is the same: You're in a battle for your mind, a battle for your future, and a battle to do and be all that God has in store for you. Never forget, your Father is by your side. The hard battles you're fighting will not last forever, and you're going to come out stronger on the other side.

Hard Battles: Questions for Reflection

1. What battles are you currently fighting? Are you winning or losing? Why?
2. Do you ever struggle to stay in the fight? How do you keep going even when you feel like quitting?
3. What are some things you've had to give up or lose in order to win battles?

Getting Better Through Bumps

Write down a specific "hard battle" you've been avoiding or resenting. What are the consequences of not addressing this? What are the benefits of addressing it? What practical step will you take *today* to embrace your hard battle?

CHAPTER 4

YOU HAVE TO START SOMEWHERE

(Hard Beginnings)

Over 350 years ago, London was in the throes of the Great Plague, part of a larger bubonic plague outbreak that affected much of Europe. It was a terrible pandemic—something we can all relate to now. Because of the plague, Isaac Newton moved to his family's home in the country. It was there that he saw an apple fall (or possibly was hit on the head by it, depending on who is telling the story) and formulated the concept of gravity.

Newton was fascinated with motion, gravity, and physical laws. You might remember learning about his first law of motion in junior high: *Objects at rest tend to stay at rest and objects in motion tend to stay in motion unless they are acted upon by some outward force.*[1]

This law states the obvious: Things keep doing what they're doing unless something happens to change that. If an apple is on a table, it won't move by itself. If a rock is hurtling through space, it will keep going forever. If a teenager is in bed, he will stay in bed until you start to wonder if he's still alive. Forces like gravity, air resistance, human intervention, and (in the case of teenagers) hunger are required to make things alter their trajectory.

Newton was talking about physical motion in the tangible world, but his law is a great metaphor for our behavior as humans. We tend to keep doing what we're doing unless something jolts us into beginning something new.

This is especially true when things are going well, which is why good is often the enemy of great, as we discussed earlier. "Good enough" often causes us to settle, to conform, to accept mediocrity rather than pursue greatness or excellence. We get into a routine and stop wondering whether we should raise the bar a little higher.

Until something comes along and shakes things up.

That "something" might be external motivation, like the loss of a job or an illness, or it might be internal motivation, such as curiosity, frustration, or a desire to achieve something. Either way, we need a metaphorical kick in the pants once in a while in order to step out of our comfort zones and try new things.

Are you in the process of beginning anything right now? Maybe you are

- Launching a new business
- Starting a family
- Going back to school
- Getting back into the dating scene
- Changing careers halfway through life
- Moving to a new city or country
- Learning a new skill or hobby
- Embarking on a fitness journey
- Writing a book or starting a creative project
- Purchasing a home
- Conquering a fear
- Starting therapy
- Checking into rehab
- Transitioning to retirement

It's an exciting time filled with possibilities and opportunities, but it's also low-key terrifying. Beginnings are rarely easy, and often they are downright hard. There is a risk to run and a price to pay. You might feel vulnerable and afraid. What if you fail? What if it doesn't work out like you hoped? What if you let everyone down? What if you make a fool of yourself? Is it worth the risk, or is it better to never try and never fail?

"Hard beginnings" are about starting new things and going new directions, and they require resilience. We have to get better at beginnings because life is full of them. If we don't have the strength and wisdom we need as we step into the unknown, we'll simply be carried along forever by our own inertia.

Overcoming Inertia

Often the hardest part of reaching a goal is getting started. It's overcoming that inertia Newton described.

Beginning something unfamiliar can feel vulnerable and overwhelming, so we simply don't start. We make excuses. We busy ourselves with other things. We make tentative plans but never carry them out. We remain stuck, unsure where or how or when to start.

That's not how I want to live, and I'm sure you don't want that either. I know I can't complete everything I desire in the next three days, but I also know that time isn't slowing down, and I have a lot of unfulfilled dreams. How sad would it be to let life pass me by simply because I couldn't overcome inertia and take that first small step?

You could probably make a list right now of things you should do or want to do but haven't done yet, for whatever reason. Without judging yourself, take a moment to consider why you haven't done those things. Is it a lack of time, resources, or know-how? Is it fear or laziness or disorganization? Is there too much opposition? Have you never tried, or did you try and give up at some point?

The point here is self-reflection, not self-condemnation. You can't condemn yourself into being better. The guilt trip tactic might work at first, but it's a terrible long-term force. Rather than criticizing yourself, notice where you are "at rest" and think about what force is needed to get moving.

Let me share a few suggestions to overcome inertia and embrace hard beginnings.

1. Listen to the right voices.

In any new endeavor, the first step is often the hardest one because you must overcome the voices of a thousand critics—most of whom are inside your own head. Those inner critics include fear, self-doubt, shame, and pain from past failures. Along with those voices, you might have to deal with people in your life (often well-meaning ones) who speak from a place of criticism and doubt. They think they know you, but they only know the version of you they've seen. Deep inside, you know you are called to outgrow that version of yourself.

Get counsel and advice from other people (aka hard asks) and pay attention to the concerns in your head. But don't let those things have the final word. God gets that. And if he's calling you forward, listen to his voice. Give the bulk of your attention to the voices of peace, faith, and wisdom.

2. Don't underestimate the power of the first step.

You might remember Neil Armstrong's famous words as he stepped from the lunar module onto the surface of the moon in 1969: "That's one small step for man, one giant leap for mankind." He knew that the step itself signified a much larger triumph. It was the beginning of humanity's exploration of a new world.

It's all too easy to underestimate the importance of the tiny steps we're taking. However, what matters most isn't the size of the steps but the direction. Every step forward is progress. When Israel was rebuilding the temple and city that had been destroyed, God told them, "Do not despise these small beginnings" (Zechariah 4:10 NLT). Are you despising any small beginnings in your life? Have you hesitated to start something because it seems too small, too insignificant, too impossible?

If so, stop underestimating the power of that first step. What do you want to do? Where do you want to go? What is the next dream you'd like to pursue? Take the first step! It's one small step today, but it's a giant leap for your future.

3. Don't *overestimate* the first step either.

Sometimes we despise small beginnings, but other times we exaggerate the risk they entail. We don't want to take a step until we have the entire plan figured out, turned into a PowerPoint deck, and fully funded—as if life were that predictable!

While planning is important, if you wait until conditions are perfect, you'll never take that crucial first step. Here's yet another nugget of wisdom from Ecclesiastes: "Whoever watches the wind will not plant; whoever looks at the clouds will not reap" (11:4). The author wasn't advocating that farmers ignore the weather. Instead, he was saying that if you look hard enough, you'll always find reasons to wait. Sometimes you just have to take a risk.

Remember, the first step is just that—a step. It's not as intimidating as it seems, and it doesn't cost as much as you might think. Don't overthink it. Enjoy it.

4. Make plans, but trust God.

In general, before taking a big first step, you should make plans. Plans are good, necessary, responsible—and notoriously unreliable. As I said, life is unpredictable, which means plans can take you only so far.

Proverbs says, "In their hearts humans plan their course, but the LORD establishes their steps" (16:9). I love that. God doesn't tell us not to have hopes, dreams, ideas, strategies, or plans. He just reminds us that he is sovereign over all those things, and our plans may or may not be his. There is peace and rest in that understanding because you don't have to figure it all out before you start. Yes, you should have a budget, a vision, and the best strategies possible—but trust God more than you trust those things.

The good news is you can adjust your course as you go. Life is mostly trial and error anyway. Embrace the ambiguity, stop expecting never to make a mistake, and know that God will help you figure things out as you go along.

Only Time Will Tell

One of the difficult things about beginnings, as we saw earlier, is that they can feel underwhelming. They often seem so small and insignificant that it's tempting to look down on them. And if we look down on them, we might give up on them.

I think if we could see hard beginnings the way God does, we'd feel and act a lot differently. He is outside of time, so he knows what's coming—and he's excited about it. He's making plans for it. He's breathing upon it. God said through the prophet Isaiah, "I make known the end from the beginning" (46:10). He can see exactly what today's small beginning is going to become in ten, twenty, or a hundred years, and that long-term perspective makes all the difference. If you could foresee the return on today's investment like he does, can you imagine how excited and inspired you would be, and how motivated you'd feel to overcome obstacles?

If you're struggling with a hard beginning in some area, try asking, "What could this look like ten years from now?" You can't fully answer that question, but at least it will get you thinking outside the small box of what your eyes can see today.

The vulnerable, risky, nerve-wracking step you're taking today is going to pay off. It's like a tiny sapling planted in the ground that will grow into a tree and bear fruit for decades to come. Someday you'll look back on today and thank yourself for overcoming the obstacles and planting this tree.

The fact that you can't perfectly predict the outcome of today's small step is exciting. What good results will come from your present actions? How will this step change your life? Whom will it benefit? How will it change the course of your family for generations to come? What doors will it open? Only time will tell—but the potential is thrilling.

The future is in God's hands, not yours, but he asks you to be faithful today to take that first step. Sometimes we look at people who seem to have great success and feel envious of their "good luck." They have a prosperous business or a wonderful family or great influence and fame or amazing athletic ability. It's tempting to see their current state and assume they arrived there easily, almost overnight. But when you talk to them, you always discover the same thing: They've been working at this for a long time. They started small, they faced risk, they went through dark days, they sacrificed much—but today, it's all worth it.

Twenty years from now, what beginning will you look back on and say, "It was worth it"? Imagine that for a moment. Visualize a future version of yourself reaping the benefits of today's hard work. Someday you're going to say, "I'm so glad I didn't put that thing off. I was scared, but I started anyway. I was vulnerable, but I didn't let that stop me. It was challenging, but I pushed through. It was hard work, but I persevered."

The good news is that once you get things started, they often take on a life of their own. Like Newton's "objects at rest," it's going to take some concentrated effort to get something moving. But once it's moving, it tends to keep moving. You'll have to steer it and turn it and tweak it, but the hardest part is getting started.

Don't let inertia define your life. You have to start somewhere, sometime, and somehow—why not today?

Hard Beginnings: Questions for Reflection

1. What is something you started a decade or more ago that is bearing good fruit today? What would you tell a younger version of yourself if you could travel back in time to when you were just getting started?
2. What are some "beginnings" that you are starting now or intend to start soon? What is the hardest part about getting started? How are you dealing with that?
3. Are there things you know you need to start but you've been avoiding them? What do you think is causing that? How could you address the obstacles and take small steps forward?

Getting Better Through Bumps

Write down a specific "hard beginning" you've been avoiding or resenting. What are the consequences of not addressing this? What are the benefits of addressing it? What practical step will you take *today* to embrace your hard beginning?

CHAPTER 5

THE POWER OF THE PIVOT

(Hard Changes)

If you're not a basketball fan, it's possible you've never heard of Jerry West. You've probably seen him though or, at least, his silhouette: It's the NBA logo.

Jerry West passed away in June 2024 after a basketball career that spanned an astonishing sixty years. As a player, he was an All-Star for every single one of the fourteen seasons he played with the Lakers. Because of his reputation for making crucial shots and plays under pressure, he was nicknamed "Mr. Clutch." When he retired from basketball at the age of thirty-six, he had already left an indelible mark on the game.

But Jerry West didn't really retire.

He pivoted.

And as it turned out, his greatest influence on basketball came *after* his playing days ended. He was a coach and then a scout for a while, until eventually he became the general manager of the Lakers. That's where the second act of his life really began. Over the next two decades, he put together teams that won six championships, working with players like Magic Johnson, Kareem Abdul-Jabbar, Kobe Bryant, and Shaquille O'Neal. He helped create the legendary "Showtime" style of play that revolutionized modern basketball.

West later went to the Memphis Grizzlies, where he was instrumental in turning their franchise around, and from there to the Golden State Warriors and then the Los Angeles Clippers. Everywhere he went, he added value and left a mark. He spent a total of forty-five years in executive roles, and his teams won eight championship rings. He's the only player ever to have been inducted three times into the Hall of Fame.

Now, I love basketball, but that's not why I'm talking about Jerry West. His life illustrates the power of the pivot, both on and off the court. When life comes at you fast and you need to make a change, how do you respond? Do you shut down? Panic? Lash out? Freeze up? Or do you keep your cool and figure out what needs to be done to win the game?

In other words, do you know how to pivot?

Don't Panic—Pivot

We're talking about making hard changes under high pressure. These are adjustments you don't necessarily want to make, but you don't have much of a choice. Circumstances have changed, plans didn't work out, and things have shifted. You either adapt or die.

In basketball, *pivoting* involves keeping one foot stationary on the ground while moving the other foot to adjust your position. If someone passes the ball to you, you have three options: pass it, shoot it, or dribble it and move somewhere else. Pivoting is what you do while you're deciding which of those three options is best. You can't just stand there, though, because opposing players with very long arms will try to get the ball away from you the whole time. So you keep moving, you keep swiveling your body, you keep looking for a chance to pass, shoot, or break for the basket, all while protecting the most valuable of possessions: the basketball.

That's a scary place to be, by the way. You feel threatened, trapped, hemmed in. You're on the verge of getting the ball stripped or running out the shot clock. Everything is in a state of flux: It's fluid, changing, dynamic. So you pivot like the game depends on it—because it really does.

Pivoting is about creating new opportunities under pressure. It's about responding in real time to the opposition you face and adjusting as needed. It's about guarding the valuable things—your integrity, your heart, your calling, your relationships—while ducking and dodging opposing forces, all without losing sight of your goals.

You don't have to be a basketball fan to understand the metaphor here. Life comes at you fast, and you'd better be ready to adjust on the fly. You won't always have the luxury of time either. Sometimes you have to make the clutch moves when the pressure is the greatest.

This is about change. It's about adaptation. It's about responding in real time to unexpected developments. Changes in your life may not move as fast as a basketball game, but they are just as relentless—and have much higher stakes. If you're going to be a resilient person, you must learn to be an adaptable one. The two go hand in hand.

Are you this kind of person? Think about it for a moment. How do you respond when your plans don't work out? When the stakes are high and the pressure is on? When you feel trapped in a corner, not by six-foot-six basketball players but by life? Do you panic, or do you pivot?

A pivot is a relatively quick thing. You're going one way, then you realize things aren't going to end well if you keep going, so you change directions. But how do you do that successfully? Here are three things to keep in mind.

1. Pivoting should create space.

When you're forced to reevaluate your plans or adjust your expectations, start by creating space. Just as a basketball player holds the ball close and then uses his or her body and movement to clear space, so you need to give yourself time to think and room to work.

This is first about creating headspace. You might feel trapped and threatened, but don't panic. Don't give up the ball. Instead, look for ways to increase your mental and emotional space. That could be as simple as going for a walk or having a conversation with a friend. Get your feelings under control.

Once your head is in the right place, look for ways to create space in your finances, time, or whatever area is under attack. For example, if you just lost your job, create a new budget immediately. Free yourself from as many obligations as you can so you have as much financial margin as possible.

Sometimes the space you need to create is between you and your *comfort*. A desire to be at ease and free from pressure can get you into trouble. It can make you sloppy. The adrenaline and fear of high-pressure situations are a good reminder that the stakes are high and comfort is not the goal. So when you find yourself in a situation where you need to pivot, make sure you aren't trying to pivot your way back to safety or comfort.

2. Pivoting should provide protection.

When you're dealing with tough changes, your pivot should provide protection. Make sure you immediately evaluate what matters most. What do you need to hold on to, and what can be released? What is essential and what is not? The last thing you want to do is panic under pressure and blow up your health, marriage, reputation, or finances. So when you pivot, keep the ball safe.

Now, I don't mean this in a purely defensive way. Protection isn't about hanging on to the ball forever; it's about hanging on to it while you and your teammates continue to try for a basket. It's protection *with a purpose*. It's protection for a short time because you believe with all your heart that an opportunity for advancement will come.

When life attacks you, don't lose your purpose. Don't go into turtle mode, withdrawing into yourself and simply trying to survive. You have a game to play, and your goal is to *win*. Keep yourself safe while you keep working toward a win.

What does protection look like? It might mean adjusting your spending for a season so you don't go into debt or can get out of it. It might mean getting a second job to bring in extra cash. It might involve taking a class or learning a new skill so you have a backup plan. It might be adjusting your work schedule to prioritize family time if you're going through a rough time at home. It all depends on what challenge you're facing and what hard choices you're making.

Focus on taking proactive steps to stay safe and keep from losing what matters to you, but do it out of hope for the future, not fear of it. Yes, you're facing threats right now, but can you find ways to protect what's important to you while you look for ways to get unstuck?

3. Pivoting should improve your position.

Finally, pivoting is meant to lead to progress. Hopefully you come out *ahead*. It's hard to believe that's possible when you're being threatened, though. At that point, you might think survival is the best you can hope for. But God is bigger than that. He has a plan in your pivot; you just have to keep your eyes open.

Think of Joseph. That guy pivoted more than Jerry West. He went from wealth to slavery to prison to second-in-command over Egypt. He told his brothers, "You intended to harm me, but God intended it for good to accomplish what is now being done, the saving of many lives" (Genesis 50:20).

Think of Esther. She went from orphan to queen to ultimately delivering her entire nation because she was willing to put her life on the line. Her cousin and guardian told her, "And who knows but that you have come to your royal position for such a time as this?" (Esther 4:14). No matter how confusing her circumstances were, she believed God had a purpose.

Never stop believing that opportunities will open up and better days will come. The pivot may be stressful, chaotic, and uncertain, but it won't last forever, and you will come out better on the other side.

Slow It Down

So far, we've focused on the fact that pivoting often takes place under pressure, which is true. However, pressure doesn't always mean urgent problems or quick decisions. As a matter of fact, the best pivots often happen when we slow down.

Sometimes on the basketball court you'll hear a coach yell "Slow it down!" to the players. Usually this is when things have gotten a little heated and people have been scrambling. The coach wants the team to lower the temperature a little, stop acting on adrenaline, and go back to running the plays they've practiced. You don't win games by reacting to emergencies. You win by controlling the pace and play.

The same holds true in life. You shouldn't always be in a state of emergency, pivoting at the last second to avoid disaster. Instead, get ahead of the game. Look ahead and predict what's coming, then prepare for it.

This kind of pivot is not about reacting to emergencies but rather about creating opportunities. However, you won't see those opportunities unless you slow down long enough to regain control.

In Jerusalem, there is an ancient stairway called the Southern Steps that leads up to the Temple Mount. Jesus himself would have used this stairway when he visited the temple, especially during great pilgrimage festivals. The unique thing about the Southern Steps is that the steps are not uniform. They vary in both height and depth, which makes them tricky to climb. You can't put your brain on autopilot like you would for a normal stairway.

This arrangement was intentional, according to tradition. It caused pilgrims and worshippers to walk carefully and intentionally as they approached God. They had to slow down, pay attention, and be present.

That thought is inspiring to me. How often do we get so caught up in routine that we fail to notice where we are or where we are going? How often do we live on autopilot, carried from point A to point B by sheer muscle memory? I don't mean only in our walk with God (although that's part of it) but in every area of life. Our mind gets into a rhythm and routine that can be as difficult to break as inactivity or even more difficult if our busyness keeps us from paying attention to what needs to change. Even things like fear, pain, and abuse can become so normalized that it seems easier to live with them than to put in the work to break them. They've been part of our lives for so long they seem impossible to get rid of, or maybe we've simply stopped noticing them altogether.

Breaking out of the force of habit starts with awareness. Just like pilgrims carefully climbing a stairway to pray, we need to become hyperaware of where our feet are and where we're placing them next.

Take a moment and think about your steps. In each of the following areas, where are you today, and where are you going next? Is your current path the right one, or do you need to make some changes?

- Your walk with God
- Your marriage and/or family
- Your mental health
- Your financial picture
- Your dreams and desires for life
- Your physical body and health
- Your education or personal growth
- Your career

Were you able to define clearly where you currently are in these areas, or have you been on autopilot for so long that you hardly even know? And even more important, do you know what your next step is going to be and *why* that is your next step?

There's no judgment here. I'm not saying that your direction is wrong or that you need to change anything. But you won't know if you need to pivot until you slow down and pay attention to the steps you're taking. Don't sacrifice your potential on the altar of routine.

How do we determine when we need to break out of our routines or our comfort zones and make some hard changes? Keep these three phrases in mind.

1. Calm down.

"Hey, you need to calm down" is usually the most dangerous thing you can say to someone who is upset—especially your spouse. However, it's often good advice to give *yourself*. The Bible says, "Be still, and know that I am God" (Psalm 46:10). Something similar is found in Psalm 131:2, which reads, "I have calmed and quieted myself." There is something to be said for getting off the treadmill of life and taking a little breather. You can't go at full speed all the time.

Often, the key to getting somewhere quicker is to stop rushing forward so frantically. It seems counterintuitive, but "haste makes waste," as they say. We weren't designed to be constantly stressing and striving. Our bodies, brains, and relationships function better when we move at the pace of peace.

If you find yourself struggling to make the changes you know you need to make, try talking yourself into a calmer headspace. Breathe. Relax. Give yourself some space and show yourself some compassion. Don't try to fulfill your dreams in a day or fix all your issues in a week.

2. Pay attention.

The very act of paying attention is transformative. Awareness is often half the battle. If we just look around, we'll see more clearly what is going on, what needs to change, and what to do next.

The problem is life isn't very conducive to paying attention. It moves so quickly and shouts so loudly that it's easy to live in a blur, barely noticing the true state of things.

Calm down and pay attention. I promise you, it will make things easier. You are smart, and the Holy Spirit is with you. You'll figure out what to do. But first, you have to look around and see what is really going on.

3. Be present.

Finally, after you calm down and pay attention, choose to be present. We usually spend too much time in the *past*, lamenting our failures or longing for the good old days; or we spend too much time in the *future*, wishing for something we don't have yet. But we've been given only today. Until somebody invents time machines, we can't go backward or forward in time, so we might as well make the most of today.

This intentional focus on being present will help you overcome the comfort and familiarity of routine. It will help you remain in a state of awareness even when the pace of life picks up and things get a little chaotic. And it will help you pivot at the right time and in the right way.

Where are you at right now? What can you enjoy today? Who is with you in your life journey? Whom do you love, and who loves you? What resources are in your hand? What skills, passions, and talents do you have? What are you thankful for? What gifts has God given you? What opportunities are in front of you?

Asking yourself questions such as these will calm you down, bring your attention back to the world around you, and help you stay present and grounded in reality. Life is big and fast and loud, but you can take ownership of your pace and trajectory.

Hard changes are a part of life because the world is too big for any of us to predict or control. We're going to have to respond to things that are outside our comfort zone, our experience, our training, or our knowledge.

That's okay because even in the most unexpected circumstances, God is with us. He's not taken by surprise. He saw this situation coming a long time ago. He knows where we need to take a risk, make a choice, follow a dream, try out an idea, or pursue a passion. He is leading us down new paths and opening new doors.

Don't panic. Instead, trust God, get creative, and pivot. You've got a game to win.

Hard Changes: Questions for Reflection

1. Think of a time you had to pivot in your life. What emotions did you experience? How did you handle the changes? What did you learn?
2. Are you currently pivoting or changing in any area? How are you creating space? How are you protecting what's important? How are you improving your position?
3. Is it difficult for you to slow down, pay attention, and be present? Why or why not? How could you improve in any or all of these areas?

GETTING BETTER THROUGH BUMPS

Write down a specific "hard change" you've been avoiding or resenting. What are the consequences of not addressing this? What are the benefits of addressing it? What practical step will you take *today* to embrace your hard change?

CHAPTER 6

NOT YOUR HILL TO DIE ON

(Hard Compromises)

The word *compromise* gets a bad rap sometimes. It is often seen as a negative, a loss, an indication of weakness or cowardice. "No compromise!" is a rallying cry for people fighting for justice, and their willingness to pay any price in order to see change is admired and applauded.

I get that. There are certain things that should not be compromised no matter what. I also understand, though, that you can't die on every hill.

Not long ago I read a fascinating article about the drafting of the US Constitution. (Well, it was fascinating for me because I am a bit of a history nerd.) In those formative, chaotic, fragile times, compromise was not only necessary, but it was good. It led to an outcome that strengthened the nation.

The year was 1787, and the United States was only eleven years old. It had become clear that the national government needed to be strengthened, since the states that formed the Union were only loosely connected and the whole thing was in danger of falling apart. So a Constitutional Convention was held in Philadelphia, and the various states sent delegates with the goal of crafting a constitution that would unite all the states.

But there was a problem. The states couldn't agree on how to make sure each state was fairly represented in the national government, primarily because there was a rift between the bigger states and the smaller ones.

The plan proposed by the larger states, the Virginia Plan, called for a two-chamber legislature with representation based completely on state population or financial contributions. That would have meant states with more people had greater influence. The smaller states hated the idea. They didn't want to be left out of the decision-making process on a national level, which is understandable. None of us want to be bullied or run over or feel like our voices don't count.

The smaller states proposed the New Jersey Plan, which called for a one-chamber legislature with equal representation regardless of population, size, or financial contribution. Naturally the larger states weren't on board. They didn't want states with few people and less income gaining a disproportionately large voice in making decisions, which also makes sense. The larger states represented more people, so their voice needed to carry more weight in order to reflect the demographics of the country.

The states were deadlocked, and neither side could convince the other to see things their way. Eventually, they reached what is called the Great Compromise or the Connecticut Compromise. The legislature would have two chambers: the House of Representatives and the Senate. The House would have representation based on population, and the Senate would consist of exactly two senators per state.

The compromise kept the two groups of states happy—or at least happy enough—and it's the system the United States of America still follows today. Crisis averted. They found a way to work together.[1]

Two things stand out to me about this story. First, neither side was wrong to have their requests and desires. They weren't being selfish; they were being honest. Second, in pursuit of a common good, each side had to be willing to reevaluate and relinquish some of its demands. The compromise was not easy, but it was for their own good because it was for the good of the whole, and they were part of that whole.

That's the power of compromise. It's never easy, but it brings people together rather than driving them apart.

Rethinking Compromise

The issue here is that *compromise* has multiple definitions. It can mean "an agreement or a settlement of a dispute that is reached by each side making concessions," but it can also mean "the acceptance of standards that are lower than is desirable."[2] The first is amoral: neither right nor wrong. The second is always wrong.

The Bible talks about both. For example, the "bad" form of compromise is on full display in James 4:4. "You adulterous people, don't you know that friendship with the world means enmity against God? Therefore, anyone who chooses to be a friend of the world becomes an enemy of God."

On the other hand, the "good" form of compromise is highlighted in verses such as Romans 12:18: "If it is possible, as far as it depends on you, live at peace with everyone." Another one is Philippians 2:3–4: "Do nothing out of selfish ambition or vain conceit. Rather, in humility value others above yourselves, not looking to your own interests but each of you to the interests of the others."

When it comes to making hard compromises, you have to be able to differentiate between good and bad concessions. You need to ask yourself: *Is this hard because I have to sacrifice a personal desire or preference, but ultimately it will lead to better outcomes all around? Or is this hard because I'm being forced to violate a personal conviction or ignore a valid need that I'm going to regret later?*

Too often, we give in when we should stand up, and we fight when we should settle. We need to get our values straight. What is worth fighting for, and what is not? When should we *stand* our ground, and when should we look for *common* ground?

This is precisely why compromises are hard—not just because they involve giving something up, but because they involve peering into the motivations and desires of our hearts. When you're facing a compromise, you're forced to evaluate what really matters to you. And the answer isn't always something you're proud of.

Compromises are also hard because they involve conflict, and usually that conflict is about something important. If you and your significant other disagree over where to eat lunch, you can probably reach a compromise quickly. But if you're arguing about whether to move to another state or make some other major life change, the stakes get a lot higher and emotions run a lot deeper.

I remember my parents having discussions that they called "intense fellowship." They weren't arguments, per se, and I don't recall my dad ever raising his voice, but my parents were clearly not on the same page about something. They would talk it out—intensely—until they reached an agreement.

On more than one occasion, my dad sat beside me after one of those discussions and said, "Son, here's a lesson for when you get married. You can win the argument or win the battle, but not both." My takeaway was that even if he was right, he still wanted to be good. He might compromise his stance on a topic, but he wouldn't compromise his integrity, his love for my mom, or the unity of the family.

What are you willing to compromise? In arguments, do you fight to be right because your ego is running the show, but end up harming relationships that matter far more? In negotiations, do you stand up for your preferences and goals, but then give in to the temptation to lie, cheat, or steal to get what you want? In projects at work, do you push to do things your way but end up compromising the overall success of the endeavor because you won't listen to others? In debates or differences of opinion, do you dig in your heels and demand the last word, thereby compromising the learning and growth you should experience?

The question isn't *whether* you will compromise; it's *what* you will compromise and *why* you compromise it. Those are questions only you can answer.

The Third Way

The goal of a healthy compromise isn't to impose one person's way on another. If both people are relatively good, smart, and experienced, yet you still see things differently, there's probably a good reason why. It's likely both of you bring a unique but equally valid viewpoint to the table.

Rather than one of you being "right," recognize that you are both partially right and together you can find a solution that is better than either idea being presented. This third way is the creative result of the two of you working together. It's an idea neither would have reached without humbly and carefully listening to the other.

When my wife and I have "intense fellowship" of our own, we try to keep this in mind. We agreed a long time ago that when we disagree, it's not about her winning or me winning, but about *us* winning. We make better decisions for our finances, our son, our home, our jobs, our health, and our marriage when we work to merge our differences and create something new.

You can carry that same principle into any relationship. Resist the urge to make people who disagree with you the enemy. Their differences are a gift. They might be exactly what you need to avoid dangers you haven't even seen. The more different you are, the more you'll be able to see each other's blind spots, watch each other's backs, and complement each other's gifts.

But you won't accomplish that if you put on your boxing gloves and go to your corners, waiting for the bell to ring so you can clobber each other for another round. You have to stop treating conflicts like fights to be won and instead make them opportunities to create.

Whom are you most at odds with right now? Who is the most

challenging, difficult, complicated person you know? Picture them. Imagine your main points of disagreement. Then ask yourself: *What do I need to learn about this person? What can he or she teach me? What does that person see that I need to learn? What can I do to draw closer to him, to understand her, to be at peace with that person?*

You can't control others' reactions, but you can control your perspective. Often, that's all it takes. Whether you're drafting a national constitution or just trying to work together or live together, healthy compromise is your friend.

When to Compromise—and When Not To

So when is it okay or even desirable to seek a middle ground, and when should you stand your ground? And if you do need to make some concessions and look for a win-win solution, how do you do that? Each scenario you face is a case-by-case decision, so nobody can give you a precise list of when compromise is right or wrong. However, some criteria can help you navigate the decision-making process.

What follows are questions I ask myself when I'm trying to discern if, how, and when I need to look for a compromise. These are things I think about no matter what the context is—a disagreement with my wife, a conversation with my son, a relationship with a friend, a problem at work, or even a dream or desire I'm struggling to fulfill.

1. What does God say?

This should be your go-to question in every area of life, but it's especially valuable when you are trying to decide what your nonnegotiables should be. Pray about it. Study the Bible. Consider what you know about God's values and will. Pay attention to whether the Holy Spirit is leading you in a particular direction.

The Bible says, "For those who are led by the Spirit of God are the children of God" (Romans 8:14). Your first consideration in any disagreement or problem should not be *What makes the most financial sense?* or *What do I think should happen?* but rather *What does God have to say about this?* Just asking yourself the question is often enough to unravel tough decisions and bring clarity regarding how to move forward.

2. Will this matter in eternity?

In other words, in the grand scheme of things, does this really matter that much? This is about gaining perspective. Sometimes the hills we defend so passionately are just mounds of dirt we need to walk away from in order to pursue what really matters. We've made mountains out of molehills, then we've declared ourselves king of the mountain. But it's still just a glorified molehill that we should have walked away from a long time ago.

If we spend our time defending a hill God never intended for us, we won't experience the hills he has planned. We'll miss out on the elevation gain and the advancement that he intended.

When you're dealing with a complex issue, try getting a higher, more eternal perspective. Life is too short to waste time fighting over things that won't matter in a month, much less in eternity.

3. What are my motives?

Motives matter because they skew our perspectives and actions in ways we often don't even notice. When you find yourself in a complex situation and you're wondering whether to stand up for what you want or look for a compromise, take a moment to check your heart. Are you listening to wisdom? Or are you listening to ego, fear, greed, habit, ignorance, or some other unreliable voice?

If your motives are primarily selfish, that's a big red flag. It doesn't mean you're wrong, but it does mean you're prejudiced. This happens to everyone from time to time, but you don't have to stay there. If you're humble and brave enough to recognize your built-in bias toward self, you can make a conscious decision to override that default and include the needs of others in your decision, as Philippians 2:4 says: "not looking to your own interests but each of you to the interests of the others."

On the other hand, if your motives are primarily focused on the good of the group, you can have more confidence in your ideas. You still shouldn't assume you're infallible, but at least you can know that your decisions are not overly biased and skewed by self-interest.

4. What would love do?

The rule of love should be the defining criteria in any decision. If you choose to see any difference, conflict, or argument through the lens of love, you immediately bring both sides closer. You'll look for ways to connect, to learn, to share, to grow together.

Things like fear, greed, and offense polarize us, and they make healthy compromise practically impossible. Love has a way of disarming those things. Love is patient, kind, generous, forgiving, wise, and constant. It overcomes selfishness. It perseveres until it finds a solution. It seeks understanding rather than control. It seeks the good of all, and it treats others as oneself.

If you're facing a complicated situation and you don't know what to do, ask yourself what love would do, then do that.

5. What would godly wisdom say?

When you're dealing with someone with an opposing viewpoint, it's easy to let the conflict escalate. People tend to get polarized and treat each other as enemies. That's not God's way. He calls us to walk in wisdom and to work together in peace and unity. Notice how James described the wisdom that comes from the world versus the wisdom of God:

> If you harbor bitter envy and selfish ambition in your hearts, do not boast about it or deny the truth. Such "wisdom" does not come down from heaven but is earthly, unspiritual, demonic. For where

you have envy and selfish ambition, there you find disorder and every evil practice. But the wisdom that comes from heaven is first of all pure; then peace-loving, considerate, submissive, full of mercy and good fruit, impartial and sincere. (3:14–17)

Two forms of wisdom are described here. One is earthly and demonic, and it leads to confusion, chaos, envy, and greed. The other is heavenly, and it produces peace and other good fruit. When you're working on a hard compromise, ask yourself, *Which path reflects the wisdom from above?*

6. What is authentic to me?

Authenticity is about honesty with yourself. It's about respecting your values, conscience, and priorities. If you want to avoid making bad compromises, learn to be honest with yourself. What is truly valuable to you? What are your nonnegotiables?

This is a process of self-discovery. You have to learn more about what truly matters to you. Some things that are important to others might not be important to you, and certain things that others couldn't care less about might be central to who you are.

This isn't a "my way or the highway" approach at all. It's a humble, self-aware approach where you are confident enough to say, *This matters to me. I can't change this without being untrue to myself.*

7. How can we add value to each other?

Yes, it's complicated to work with other people, but that complication is a gift. You are making each other *stronger* by working together because you each bring unique perspectives, experiences, and talents to the table.

This is a matter of perspective. Rather than framing hard compromises as "giving in" or "losing" something, look at them as a necessary part of healthy collaboration. Instead of resenting the fact that you don't get your way, celebrate the fact that the third way you are agreeing to is a stronger option than either of you could have come up with on your own.

Taking this perspective is a choice, and it's a hard one at times. In the heat of a disagreement, it's all too easy to dig in our heels and argue for our plans as if God himself engraved them on a tablet on Mount Sinai, right next to the other commandments. But if we're honest with ourselves, we're usually not standing on Mount Sinai, defending divine revelation; we're standing on a little hill of our own making, defending our egos or our ideas. God isn't asking us to die on that hill or even defend it. He's asking us to let down our guards, lower our weapons, and invite people into our worlds so we can all grow together.

We're better together. That was the reason the founders of the United States fought so hard to keep those thirteen fragile colonies together, even when they had to make some difficult compromises along the way. Rather than letting disagreements and differences split us apart, we need to embrace the complexity of working together and stay with the conversations that will lead to better collaboration. On the other side of hard compromises, we'll find safety, companionship, and unity.

Hard Compromises: Questions for Reflection

1. Can you remember a time you had to compromise (in a good way)? What happened? How did you navigate it, and what were the results?
2. Does it tend to be easy or hard for you to work together with someone until you reach a compromise? Why? How have you grown in this area over time?
3. Describe your process when you are at odds with someone and you need to reach an agreement. How do you think, act, and talk to that person? What criteria do you use to evaluate different solutions and eventually find common ground?

GETTING BETTER THROUGH BUMPS

Write down a specific "hard compromise" you've been avoiding or resenting. What are the consequences of not addressing this? What are the benefits of addressing it? What practical step will you take *today* to embrace your hard compromise?

CHAPTER 7

WE NEED TO TALK

(Hard Confessions)

"We need to talk" is one of those phrases that should come with a trigger warning. My wife texts this to me regularly, and it always scares me to death. At least 90 percent of the time it has nothing to do with me, and even when it does mean I messed up, it's usually something like "Dishes go in the dishwasher, not the sink." Regardless, my mind always races to worst-case scenarios when I read that text message. Why? Because over the course of my life, I've made my share of mistakes and let more than a few people down, and I've found that "we need to talk" is often the start of a difficult conversation.

Has someone ever said that to you? Maybe you didn't mean to do anything wrong or hurt them, but you messed up. You hurt their feelings, you harmed them in some way, you neglected a responsibility, or you let them down. They want to talk about it—and by "talk," they mean you need to apologize.

And they're right. You know it, even if you don't want to admit it. You messed up, and they deserve an apology.

That's never fun. Confession is hard. Nobody likes to admit they were wrong. The act of stating your error out loud feels humbling, vulnerable, embarrassing, and awkward.

But it's also so *freeing*. That's the thing you have to understand about hard confessions: On the other side of humility and honesty, you'll find genuine freedom and healing.

It's a hard path, but it's a healing path.

Confess and Be Healed

To *confess* simply means to admit or acknowledge something you've done wrong. It can be something you did to harm someone else or a sin you've hidden inside.

Often, confession can be as simple as saying, "You're right, I'm sorry. I did leave dirty dishes in the sink." Rather than defending or denying the issue, you own your actions and move forward. Other times, confession is more complex because you have to wrestle deeply with the intentions of your heart and the results of your wrong actions. In those cases, confession might be just the beginning of a long process of restoration.

Regardless of the size or nature of your mistake, confession is the key to beginning the healing process. Proverbs 28:13 teaches, "Whoever conceals their sins does not prosper, but the one who confesses and renounces them finds mercy."

Recently I read about South Africa's transition out of apartheid back in the nineties. Apartheid was a form of government that was blatantly, intentionally racist. The system classified citizens into racial groups (white, black, colored, and Indian) and enforced strict laws that dictated where people could live, work, and socialize based on their race. Only white citizens could vote, and non-white South Africans were subjected to inferior treatment in all aspects of life: education, health care, employment, and more. This led to terrible human rights abuses that lasted for decades.

Eventually, South Africa came to terms with its legacy and transitioned from apartheid to democracy under the leadership of figures such as Nelson Mandela and Desmond Tutu. In 1995, after apartheid ended, the Truth and Reconciliation Commission (TRC) was established to promote national unity and reconciliation by confronting the human rights violations that had taken place.[1] The commission conducted public hearings—broadcast on radio and television—where victims, perpetrators, and witnesses could testify about their experiences. The goal was to help the nation address the atrocities of the past and begin a healing journey.

The process was painful but powerful. All sides came together, told the truth, and reconciled wrongs and differences in order to become a united nation.

To my knowledge, South Africa's TRC is the only example of nationwide repentance in modern history. While confession didn't undo the damage of the past, it was a necessary step in the healing process.

Without honesty, nobody can move forward. Both victims and perpetrators will be stuck in the past. Whether as a nation or as individuals, we can't heal from a history we won't acknowledge. "Out of sight, out of mind" doesn't work when we're talking about hurts and offenses.

I'm not referring only to racial reconciliation, although that's an ongoing need. This is about any interpersonal relationship that has suffered harm. Maybe you are the victim, or maybe you are the perpetrator, or maybe it was a bit of both. Maybe the harm happened ten years ago, or maybe it's still happening today. Maybe it was betrayal, dishonesty, abuse, an insult, a broken promise, violence, hurtful words, false accusations, or theft.

As humans, we are far from perfect. None of us can claim never to have hurt someone, and none of us is exempt from being hurt. That doesn't justify hurting each other, but it does point to the need for honesty and repentance.

Take a moment and consider your own life. Have you done things to hurt others that you need to confess and address? While it's tempting to quickly answer no or to say "yes, but they deserved it" or "yes, but there's no hope for reconciliation," don't rush to answer this. Sit with it for a while. Let the Holy Spirit speak to you.

Heartfelt apologies can work miracles. You might be one confession away from rebuilding a bridge you thought was destroyed forever.

Mean It When You Say It

Honesty is the heart and soul of confession: bringing what is hidden into the light so it can be healed. If we are willing to admit the part we played in the offense or the harm that was done, we've taken the first step in moving from a posture of defensiveness to one of restoration.

This is more than a superficial, flippant "Sorry, I messed up." We've probably all been on the receiving end of an insincere apology, and there's nothing healing about it. It's insulting. If you ever fought with siblings or cousins as a kid and an adult made you all apologize to one another, you know what I'm talking about. You *said* sorry to each other, but you didn't mean it.

The kind of honesty we expect from each other (and God expects of us) starts on the inside, and it involves speaking the truth on three levels.

1. Be honest with yourself.

This is the first step, and it might be the hardest of them all. Often we've convinced ourselves that we are innocent victims in a particular scenario. Our brains are all too happy to provide us with a list of reasons why the offense isn't that big of a deal or why it's all someone else's fault.

Honesty with yourself is about owning your role in the conflict or problem. You have to peer into the depths of your heart and replace hate with love, anger with forgiveness, and pride with humility. As long as you're defending yourself in your own mind, you'll be closed to the voice of God and the voice of love.

You probably know the story of King David and Bathsheba in the Bible. David was a mighty warrior who started out defeating the giant

Goliath years earlier. One day, instead of leading his troops when they went into battle, he stayed in his palace. He ended up sleeping with a woman named Bathsheba, the wife of one of his soldiers. She became pregnant, and to cover up what he had done, David secretly ordered that her husband be killed. Then he married Bathsheba.

God sent the prophet Nathan to confront David, who finally confessed and repented. Psalm 51 is David's famous psalm of repentance. However, there were still serious consequences for David that lasted the rest of his life.

David's biggest giant wasn't Goliath; it was secret sin. And his greatest losses weren't on the battlefield; they were in the palace. Because he didn't deal with his own temptation and lust the right way, he ended up creating a chain of events that destroyed several lives.

For us, the same principle can be true. Secret giants are the most dangerous ones. Nobody sees them, nobody knows what we're facing, nobody can help us, and nobody can hold us accountable. David was a great man, but his inability to be honest with himself created massive fallout.

Don't be afraid of facing the truth about yourself. The truth may hurt, but it will always set you free.

2. Be honest with God.

Once you recognize you made a mistake or need help in some area, go straight to God. He's your best source of wisdom, peace, and guidance.

A few years ago I broke my index finger. The pain level was through the roof, and I knew instantly that something was wrong. I rushed to the hospital. When the ER doctor saw me, I was hunched over, holding my hand and protecting it. The pain was so high that I didn't even want the doctor to get close. He said, "Let me see it so I can help you."

My body refused. It didn't ask my permission either. It wanted to keep my finger covered so it wouldn't hurt any worse than it already did. Obviously that was a problem because the doctor couldn't do what he needed to do to help me. I had to override my self-protective posture in order to get help.

Notice I had two problems, not just one. The first was that I'd busted my finger. That was obvious. The second was that I had adopted a defensive posture. I was covering up what needed to be healed.

We do something similar in life. We have a problem, but instead of dealing with it, we deny it. We defend it. We hide it. We protect it. We justify it. We anesthetize it with bad habits or addictions. But if we don't reveal the areas that are broken, it's impossible for God to mend them the way he desires to. Something that should have injured us once ends up injuring us for a lifetime if we don't uncover it and let God deal with it. Confession is painful, but it's not as painful as staying wounded forever.

The key is to change our posture. Rather than hunching over the parts of our lives that need attention, we need to open ourselves up to God and allow him to begin the healing process. Defensiveness won't help, but openness will.

3. Be honest with others.

If being honest with yourself is the hardest part of confession, being honest with others is a close second. This is where you go to the person you hurt, apologize for what you did, and seek restoration of the relationship.

The hard part of this is swallowing your pride. You are naturally going to want to defend yourself, to blame the other person, or both. Instead, decide to be completely open and honest about your own mistakes. Hopefully the other person responds with humility and openness, but you can't control that. All you can control is yourself.

The good news is that confession and restoration create a stronger relationship than ever. Disagreements and offenses are going to happen, but if you can push through the pain and heal the wounds, you'll create a stronger, more intimate, more honest relationship than before.

When I broke my finger, the doctor told me that once the bone grew back around the break, it would be the strongest part of my bone, and it would be less likely to break in that spot again. In the same way, a healed relationship is stronger than ever because you both learned from the situation (we hope, anyway), and the act of working toward reconciliation will unite your hearts.

Full honesty—with yourself, God, and others—is the essence of confession, and it's the key to finding healing. Don't settle for half-truths, partial confessions, or fake apologies. With courage and humility, become an open book, a person with nothing to hide and no one to fear.

When you're committed to full honesty and transparency, "we need to talk" doesn't have to be a terrifying phrase. It will probably make your mind race a little as you wonder what the person wants to talk about. But if you have no secrets to hide and if you're willing to humbly listen and learn when someone points out an error, then hard confessions become a little easier and a lot more liberating.

You don't even have to wait for someone else to bring something to your attention. As soon as you become aware of something that's lurking beneath the surface, bring it to light.

Ask yourself: *Do I need to talk about something? Where am I not being fully honest with myself, God, or others? Am I hiding anything or making excuses for wrong behavior or telling less than the truth in any area?*

Develop a habit of truth-telling and confession, and you'll discover freedom, healing, and better relationships.

Hard Confessions: Questions for Reflection

1. Can you think of a time when you hid something you should have confessed? How did that work out? What negative effects did you experience?
2. Can you think of an instance when you confessed and repented for a mistake you made? What emotions did you feel before, during, and after that confession? What did the experience teach you?
3. Consider your life right now. Is there anything hidden that needs to be brought to light? What steps could you take to make that happen?

Getting Better Through Bumps

Write down a specific "hard confession" you've been avoiding or resenting. What are the consequences of not addressing this? What are the benefits of addressing it? What practical step will you take *today* to embrace your hard confession?

CHAPTER 8

FOOL AROUND AND FIND OUT

(Hard Consequences)

My childhood hero was Indiana Jones. He was the pinnacle of everything I aspired to be when I grew up. When I was seven or eight years old, I even dressed like him, including the leather jacket and hat. What I didn't have—and what I wanted with all my heart—was a whip. That was on my Christmas list for three years straight. For two years my parents said no, but when I was nine, they finally gave in. That Christmas was the happiest day of my young life.

My dad gave me two rules. First, don't hit my sisters. Second, don't swing from a tree branch. The next day, I went outside to play with my whip. Naturally the first thing I lassoed was a tree branch. The rope wrapped around and held tight. I tugged on it. It was solid. The temptation was too much, so I picked up my feet and launched myself through the air.

Somewhere mid-swing, the lasso broke. I have a vivid memory of flying/falling straight toward a two-by-four board with a nail sticking out of it on the ground. The nail punctured my sneaker and my foot. It went in so deeply that I couldn't get it out. I had to limp into the house with a two-by-four nailed to my foot, then wait for my parents to get home.

When my dad walked into the house, he took one look at me and said, "You lassoed a tree, didn't you?" I nodded. There was no sense denying it.

My dad wasn't a big fan of taking us to the hospital, so he took care of my foot himself. He pulled out the nail, poured alcohol on the wound, pulled a white sock over it, and duct-taped the sock to my foot. I healed just fine, but I never got another whip.

I fooled around and found out, as they say. I'm sure you've heard the phrase, or a variation of it, which means if you do something stupid, you'll experience the consequences.

You probably don't have to think too hard to remember a "fool around and find out" moment in your own life. The error in judgment was momentary; the consequences were not. This is such a common part of human experience that we have countless ways to describe it:

- Reap what you sow.
- Face the music.
- Pay the piper.
- Learn the hard way.
- What goes around comes around.
- Actions have consequences.
- You made your bed, now lie in it.
- If you play with fire, you get burned.

Consequences are a normal part of life. While that doesn't excuse dumb decisions like swinging from a tree branch with a toy whip, it does remind us that we need to learn how to handle these hard consequences in a way that moves us forward.

We shouldn't view hard consequences as merely punishment for the past. Rather, they are motivation for the future. We need to change our focus. Learning the hard way should be more about "learning" than about "hard."

Learning the Hard Way

We have to learn from our mistakes. If we do, the pain works for us. If we don't, the pain is wasted.

Pain isn't good or bad. It simply exists. It's what we do with it that matters. If anything, pain is a positive thing because it motivates us to change things that are broken. Unfortunately, humans tend to need the discomfort of hard consequences to make needed adjustments.

You might remember Volkswagen's infamous Dieselgate scandal a few years ago. Environmental agencies discovered the company had installed a "defeat device" on millions of cars worldwide. This device consisted of software that could detect when a car was being tested for emissions and would immediately lower emissions levels to pass the test. Once the test was over, the cars would automatically go back to their normal state, which meant emission levels up to forty times the legal limit.

When confronted, Volkswagen admitted to their actions. The fraud was obvious, and the consequences were both painful and public, including a fifteen-billion-dollar settlement and another fifteen billion or so in fines, repairs, and legal fees. Their CEO resigned, along with several other executives. Their reputation was deeply harmed, and they lost the trust of customers and the general public.

Over the next few months and years, Volkswagen went to work on themselves. They owned their mistakes, apologized, and committed to accountability. They formed a diverse Sustainability Council and overhauled their management structure to focus on ethical business and environmental responsibility. They also launched a major initiative to become a key player in electric vehicles.

Today, while they have not completely emerged from the shadow of the scandal, they're making strides toward becoming a better—and more honest—company than ever before. In particular, their focus on electric cars is having an industry-wide impact.[1]

Would they have made those necessary changes without being forced to? Probably not. It's easier to hide things than to fix them. When they had to pay the piper (to the tune of about thirty billion dollars), it was the wake-up call they needed.

Life has a way of forcing us to confront the consequences of our actions. The Bible says, "Do not be deceived: God cannot be mocked. A man reaps what he sows" (Galatians 6:7). That's a *good* thing. That's what we need to realize. Without consequences, we might not make the changes we need to make.

So if you're facing the results of a mistake you made, what are you going to do? You have a few options.

- You could deny it all and try to plead innocent.
- You could blame someone else.
- You could dig in your heels and insist on not changing.
- You could spiral into a dark place of shame and never try again.
- Or . . . you could accept responsibility, learn from your mistakes, and show up stronger next time.

The choice is yours. Will you learn what you need to learn? Will you change what you need to change? Will you humble yourself, consider what went wrong, and commit to growth?

If so, you'll redeem the pain. You won't take it away, but you'll give it purpose.

Stop Demonizing Mistakes

In order to learn from your mistakes, you need to have a realistic view of your own fallibility. In other words, give yourself room to be human. Most mistakes are honest ones, after all. You don't know what you don't know. So you trial-and-error your way through life, accumulating wisdom along the way.

That's normal. It's good. It's called being human.

Some of us let negative consequences affect us too deeply. We either live in shame because of a past mistake, or we live in fear of future mistakes, or both. That's too narrow a view of failure, though.

How are you supposed to learn if you can't let yourself be wrong once in a while? You've never experienced this particular stage of life. Show yourself a little compassion. You have to try new things, and often that's going to mean doing something wrong before you figure out how to do it right.

Please don't make the mistake of assuming that just because you're facing some hard consequences right now, it means you're a failure as a person. You might have failed in some way, but failure isn't the end of your story, and neither are the consequences.

Make sure you *learn*, as we mentioned earlier, but don't demonize failure itself. Don't view mistakes as unacceptable. If anything, some mistakes are desirable. They mean you're trying. Intentionally harmful or stupid acts are not a good thing, of course, but many of our mistakes are simply errors in judgment or momentary lapses. They don't define us or imprison us—they propel us.

Ironically, a company culture that didn't allow for failure and honesty was what enticed Volkswagen over to the dark side. It simply wasn't acceptable to fail to meet goals . . . so people cheated to reach goals. And it almost destroyed the company.

How often do we do the same thing? We take failure so seriously that we'll do anything to avoid it, including cheating, hiding problems, or never taking risks. But that only sets us up for more serious consequences.

Instead, let's embrace being human with all its messiness. Let's be wise and cautious, but let's also give ourselves room to fail.

How to Handle Hard Consequences

When we do face consequences that are painful, let's use them to our advantage rather than weaponizing them to condemn ourselves.

How do you do that? Let me share three simple rules.

1. Look in the mirror.

This is about taking responsibility for your role in whatever happened. We talked about hard confessions in the last chapter, and this is related. Be honest about what is going on and who is at fault. Specifically, notice where *you* are at fault because you can only change yourself.

The human tendency is to avoid accepting responsibility because it feels painful. It's only painful for a short period, though. Then it leads to freedom and greater health. Imagine if I had hidden my foot from my dad. Painful as it was to face his disappointment, it was a lot better than trying to pretend I didn't have a two-by-four nailed to my foot.

Some of us walk around with boards stuck to our feet for years. We'd rather limp than heal. We'd rather pretend we're healthy than actually become healthy.

It takes courage and humility to face the music, but the moment you acknowledge your role in a problem is the moment you get your power back.

2. Do something differently.

Realize you have to change something or you're just going to end up in this hard place again. What can you tweak? What can you try? How can you grow? Whom can you ask for help? What should you read, watch, or study?

While my dad was bandaging my foot that day, we had a conversation. He asked me, "What did you learn?" That's the attitude you need toward yourself, as we saw earlier.

Focus on what needs to be adjusted. That's the whole point of trial and error. It's meant to be an iterative process. You learn, change, try again, learn some more, and keep changing and trying and learning until you figure things out.

This is about analyzing what went wrong. If you don't do that, you're doomed to repeat your mistakes. German philosopher Georg Hegel once said something to the effect of "If there's anything we've learned from history, it's that we don't learn from history."[2] That might be the case for civilization, but it doesn't have to be true for you and me.

3. Bounce back.

Sooner or later, you have to get back in the game. Take your newfound understanding and humility and go back out there. Did you fail in business? I've been there, and it was terrible. But you know more now, so consider trying again. Did you get in a fight with your teenager and you regret some things you said? Apologize for what you said that was out of line, keep loving him or her, and keep communicating. That relationship is too important to give up on. Did you get drunk after a year of sobriety? Don't write yourself off as a hopeless addict. Seek help and try again.

You don't have to rush this. You may need to take some time to sit with repentance, grieve what happened, and work on yourself. But don't sit forever. At some point you have to try again.

The good news is you won't be the same person as before. You won't make the same mistakes or suffer the same pain. If you've figured out what went wrong, you can move forward with greater confidence than ever.

My Indiana Jones moment was decades ago, and I can laugh about it now. My foot healed. My dad forgave me. I slowly got over the loss of my whip. Time has a way of softening or even erasing many of the consequences we face.

The lessons we learn don't fade, though. They are woven into the fabric of our characters. They shape us and form us and serve us for the rest of our lives.

The pain of what you might be facing is real, and so is the pain of those you might have hurt. Those consequences are tragic, and I don't minimize them in any way. But they aren't the end of your journey. You can move forward from this. If you fooled around and found out, have faith that God will use your mistakes to propel you forward. You won't make this same mistake again. You might even help others avoid it too. You're growing stronger and wiser day by day, and even your stumbles can be steps forward.

Hard Consequences: Questions for Reflection

1. Think of a time when you "fooled around and found out." What exactly did you find out? What changes did you make? How are you a better person today because of that experience?
2. What advice would you give someone who is dealing with hard consequences?
3. Are there any areas in your life where you've messed up and now you need to "bounce back"? What is one practical step you could take this week to begin moving forward again?

GETTING BETTER THROUGH BUMPS

Write down a specific "hard consequence" you've been avoiding or resenting. What are the consequences of not addressing this? What are the benefits of addressing it? What practical step will you take *today* to embrace your hard consequence?

CHAPTER 9

SAY WHAT YOU NEED TO SAY

(Hard Conversations)

Howard Schultz was CEO of Starbucks almost from its beginning. By the time he stepped down in 2000, he had built the chain into an internationally successful brand with thirty-five hundred stores. A few years later, the company was in trouble. Sales were dropping, and stock value had fallen 42 percent. On one hand, McDonald's and Dunkin' Donuts were chipping away at their customer base; on the other, the company had made changes to its customer experience that were watering down the Starbucks experience.[1]

Schultz was brought back on as CEO in 2008. He felt that the company had strayed from its roots as a people-centered, high-quality coffee shop, and he decided to do something about it. To start with, he shut down all seventy-one hundred US stores for half a day to retrain every barista. He got a lot of pushback from that, including from the public, the media, and stockholders. Schultz told one stockholder, "I'm doing the right thing. We are retraining our people because we have forgotten what we stand for, and that is the pursuit of an unequivocal, absolute commitment to quality."[2]

Rather than addressing the company's troubles with cost cutting, layoffs, and other draconian measures, he knew he needed to get to the heart of the matter: customer experience. One employee said he expected the training to be simply a lecture, but Schultz took a different approach. He spoke honestly and directly about what the company needed to do in order to regain trust and momentum. He talked about his own experience visiting cafés in Italy and realizing that it wasn't the beans that differentiated them, but the art of each barista. He fell in love with coffee in Italy, and he wanted to bring that experience to the United States and the world.

What stands out the most to me about Schultz's espresso intervention is his willingness to have hard conversations—not hard in the sense of "sit there while I yell at you," but hard in the sense of emotional, honest, and urgent. He didn't just deal with the negative effects the company was experiencing; he spoke about the cause. Where other CEOs might have opted to spend a day focusing on metrics, milestones, profit margins, and marketing ideas, Schultz attacked the root cause of the company's decline.

In doing so, he took a hard conversation and made it a *heart* conversation.

The Heart of the Matter

In every hard conversation, we need to do the same thing Schultz did. We need to look deeper than the surface and understand what is truly going on, then boldly and directly confront the issues.

This isn't just about getting something off our chests or speaking our piece. It's about serving the *other* person by encouraging him or her to grow and improve in some way. Proverbs 27:5–6 says, "Better is open rebuke than hidden love. Wounds from a friend can be trusted, but an enemy multiplies kisses."

In general, a "hard conversation" is an interaction that involves high stakes. For example, if you are arguing with a loved one, the stakes are relational; if you're negotiating an important deal, the stakes are financial; if you're confronting someone who has hurt you, the stakes are emotional, and so on. Anytime you or the other person has something to lose, you're engaging in a hard conversation.

Most of these conversations can be grouped into one of four categories: First, some hard conversations are about *correction*. You find it necessary to tell someone where they are wrong: wrong behavior, wrong attitudes, wrong decisions, wrong words. Obviously they aren't going to enjoy being told that, which makes the conversation tricky.

Other conversations are about *resolution*. This is when you need to work out an offense or conflict with someone else. Usually, you talk through who did what to whom, and you end up asking for forgiveness, extending it, or both. That is not easy. It's emotional, vulnerable, and high-risk.

Third, some conversations are about *protection*. You may have to establish and enforce rules that keep people safe. My son was an early talker and a late walker, so when he finally started wobbling around the house, he was able to converse a little while he did it. Specifically, I remember him always asking "But why?" every time I told him not to walk down the stairs. He didn't like the rule, but it was for his own safety. Those conversations were about protection.

Finally, hard conversations might be about *understanding*. Often you'll need to work through misunderstandings or disagreements. You have to be able to listen and learn from each other in order to establish a better connection and create solutions that work for both of you.

Hard conversations are a necessary part of life. While they don't happen all the time, they happen often enough that we need to know how to deal with them. That starts by getting to the heart of the matter and addressing it head-on.

This takes time and wisdom. Don't rush into a high-stakes conversation just because your emotions are supercharged and you want to say what you're thinking. As a matter of fact, that's the worst time for a conversation like this. James said, "My dear brothers and sisters, take note of this: Everyone should be quick to listen, slow to speak and slow to become angry, because human anger does not produce the righteousness that God desires" (1:19–20).

Instead of storming into your coworker's office or your teenager's bedroom or a stranger's DMs, take time to understand what is really going on. Start by looking at yourself with humility and at the other person with empathy. Then take stock of how your relationship is working and what you could do to connect better. Finally, consider what you're trying to accomplish and find commonalities.

If you are arguing, is the issue really the issue, or is there something deeper at play? If the person seems obstinate and unchanging, is their character the problem, or is there something else happening? Until you get to the heart of the matter, you won't even know what you need to say, much less how to say it.

How to Have Hard Conversations

Once you've taken the time to do your homework, then you're ready to say what you need to say. Let me share four suggestions to make hard conversations a little easier and a lot more fruitful.

1. Lead the conversation with love.

Love should be a primary motivation behind every hard conversation. This isn't just about your needs or wants—it's about the other person too. What you are telling that person is for his or her own long-term success.

You might need to do a little work on yourself to get to this place. If you've reached a point where you know a hard conversation is needed, there's a good chance that emotions are already running high. You might be frustrated, hurt, or angry, and those emotions can sabotage your attempt to communicate with someone if you leave them unchecked.

Take time to consider the other person before you launch into your speech about how they need to change. Where is this individual coming from? What might he be struggling with? How can you serve her? How could this conversation lead to a win for both of you?

Put yourself in the other person's shoes and treat him or her as you'd want to be treated. This is empathy. It's understanding. And it's love.

2. Layer your words with grace.

Grace often carries the idea of mercy. If you give someone grace, it means you show them compassion. For example, a teacher might give a student a grace period to complete an assignment, or the teacher might not grade as hard as he or she could. Grace can also refer to class or taste. If you walk with grace or carry yourself with grace, it means you know how to behave in a way that is refined, courteous, elegant, or educated. Both meanings—mercy and class—should describe your speech during hard conversations.

Pay attention to your tone, your terms, and your timing. Speak courteously and respectfully. Instead of raining fire and brimstone on the person, demonstrate consideration for his feelings and respect for his autonomy. Proverbs says, "One who loves a pure heart and who speaks with grace will have the king for a friend" (22:11). Paul wrote, "Let your conversation be always full of grace, seasoned with salt, so that you may know how to answer everyone" (Colossians 4:6).

The manner in which you deliver the truth can have a huge impact on how it's received. Don't just plan what you want to say—plan *how* you want to say it. Determine in advance to be gracious by showing mercy and behaving with class.

3. Be unapologetically truthful.

Jesus famously told his disciples, "Then you will know the truth, and the truth will set you free" (John 8:32). Truth leads to freedom. If you are going into a difficult conversation with someone, stay focused on what is true, knowing that ultimately it will create greater liberty and stability.

We often have one of two problems here. Either we can't wait to drop a truth bomb on someone because we enjoy telling the truth a little too much, or we are unwilling to hurt their feelings and risk the relationship by being honest. Neither extreme is loving, and neither is wise.

The Bible refers to "speaking the truth in love" (Ephesians 4:15), and I think that's a good description of how we should approach hard conversations. We must speak from love, not from selfishness, ego, or ignorance—but we *must* speak.

You probably already know which end of the spectrum you tend to gravitate toward: either too quick to speak or too slow to speak. In your next hard conversation, determine to move the needle in the right direction, either by speaking a little more lovingly or a little more firmly, depending on the case.

When it's time to have one of these conversations, be clear, direct, and concise. Don't sugarcoat things. Don't be passive-aggressive. Show love and grace, but say what you need to say.

4. Be open and receptive to helpful feedback.

I can't emphasize enough that a conversation is a two-way experience. If the other person doesn't have a chance to respond, then it's not a conversation. It's a monologue. A speech. A lecture. Maybe a rant.

Because of the back-and-forth nature of conversation, you can't plan out in advance how the interaction will go. You might know how you're going to start, and you probably have an idea of the key points you want to cover, but trust me, the other person is not going to respond the way you've imagined them responding.

I often find myself rehearsing conversations in my head before they ever happen. I imagine what I'm going to say, how the other guy is going to react, and what I'll say next. It's beautiful. I always win those arguments. I always get my point across. I keep my cool, say the right thing, speak clearly, and have irrefutable arguments.

But the actual conversation never goes according to my plan. The other person invariably goes off script within thirty seconds.

That's normal. They have a brain, just as I do. They have emotions, just as I do. They have a free will, dreams, needs, fears, goals, values, and points of view, just as I do.

If you ignore that reality, you're setting the conversation up for failure. Even if you intimidate others into silence, you aren't reaching their hearts. Plus, you don't know what you don't know. If you don't give them space to tell you what they are thinking, you'll walk away from the encounter with the same blind spots and knowledge gaps as before.

Rather than delivering a speech and marching off, engage in honest dialogue. That might seem vulnerable and risky, but it's a safeguard. You need to understand their point of view. You need to hear their objections. You need to gain their trust. The best way to do that is by genuinely listening to their feedback and engaging with them on a humble, respectful level.

Keep an open mind, open hands, and an open heart. Listen to what they have to say and admit where you are wrong. Even if you are the person's leader or manager, they are still equally valuable in the eyes of God, and there are always a few things you could learn from them.

As long as you work with people, hang out with people, or are related to people, you're going to have some hard conversations. That's a good thing because on the other side of hard conversations are closer relationships and better results. And remember, next time you're at Starbucks, you can thank a hard conversation for the coffee in your hand.

Hard Conversations: Questions for Reflection

1. What is a hard conversation you've had recently? How did you prepare for it? What do you wish you had done differently, if anything?
2. If someone needs to have a hard conversation with you, how would you want him or her to approach you? What would you want his or her attitude to be? His assumptions? Her tone? His response?
3. How skilled do you think you are at hard conversations? How could you improve?

Getting Better Through Bumps

Write down a specific "hard conversation" you've been avoiding or resenting. What are the consequences of not addressing this? What are the benefits of addressing it? What practical step will you take *today* to embrace your hard conversation?

CHAPTER 10

LEARNING FROM DONKEYS

(Hard Criticism)

I've written a few books over the years, and every manuscript I've sent to my editors has come back with comments in the margins. That's the literal job description of the editorial team: to help you see and fix problem areas. They'll tell you straight up what they like and don't like about the text. I'm not just talking about the hundreds of typos and punctuation errors highlighted in red either, but the dozens of places where they suggested (strongly) that I go back to the text and try again.

That's not exactly fun. It pokes at your ego and stretches your brain as you try to understand why someone else doesn't love what you wrote or agree with what you think. Sometimes I've had to cut or rewrite entire chapters. I've been told that my jokes fell flat, that my "interesting" information was a bit boring, and that statements I thought were profound were simply confusing. They said it more nicely than that, but we all knew what they meant.

And I wouldn't have it any other way. Books are always stronger if a team of people looks at them critically and helps shape the final product.

It's the same for anything we do, in any area of life. We need help.

We need advice. We need feedback. We need counsel, critiques, coaching, correcting, editing, revising, mentoring, training, guidance, and development.

There are two reasons we need criticism. First, it reveals our blind spots. Of course, we can't see them for ourselves or they wouldn't be called blind spots. We need other people to point out the things we can't see in ourselves, or nothing will ever change. That can be awkward and uncomfortable, especially at first, because it often takes a while to truly see the things we've been blind to.

Second, criticism helps us keep growing. It's easy to get comfortable and complacent, so negative feedback is invaluable in helping us identify areas that need work. When my wife, a staff member, a friend, or a mentor tells me something that needs to change, it pushes me out of my comfort zone and sets me on a growth trajectory. That's a good thing.

A good illustration of this is coaching. In professional sports, I'm always impressed by the relationships between good players and good coaches. Usually the players are younger, stronger, and more talented than their coaches, and they often get paid far more. But no matter how good the players are, they need someone standing on the sidelines who can give them an expert outsider's perspective.

Good players listen to the feedback and make changes. If they don't, they short-circuit their own development. Whether they refuse to listen out of pride, ignorance, fear, or stubbornness, the result is the same. They miss out on a chance to improve their game.

It's the same in life, although the "coach" could be anyone from your boss to your neighbor to your kid to a stranger on the street. You *will* be the target of criticism. What will you do about it? How will you respond? Can you take criticism even when it's hard and even when it hurts?

Of course, we won't listen to constructive feedback if we think we're doing just fine on our own. I think the biggest hurdle of all when it comes to receiving criticism is our own resistance to it. We don't like to be told that we're wrong or lacking. We don't enjoy being told we need to change something, fix something, add something, learn something, or stop something.

It's a blow to our pride, for one thing. For some of us, it probably triggers feelings of shame or insecurity. I can't speak for you, but I know for me, when someone points out a flaw, it tends to bring a lot of stuff to the surface that I didn't know was there, and I have to deal with it.

That's a good thing, though. Instead of overreacting to criticism, let it help you get to know yourself better. Be teachable and coachable. It's only going to make you a stronger person.

Of course, you have to make sure you're listening to the *right* feedback because not all criticism is created equal. Some of the voices you hear are coming from the peanut gallery.

Ignore the Peanut Gallery

Around the turn of the twentieth century, theaters would sell the upper balcony seats for the lowest price. These seats were often occupied by rowdy, loud audience members who would heckle the performers and throw peanuts at them. That's where the term "peanut gallery" comes from. It means vocal but uninformed criticism.[1]

Don't listen to the peanut gallery. Don't let their words of mockery or anger faze you. They are often the loudest voices, but that doesn't make them right. It just makes them harder to ignore.

We'll talk in a moment about how to handle constructive criticism, but not all criticism is constructive. Some of it is outright destructive. There are critics out there who shouldn't have access to your head, heart, budget, or decisions. Maybe they *tell* you they should, and maybe they even *think* they should, but they shouldn't.

You can't please everyone, and you shouldn't try. It's a setup for failure. You might have heard Aesop's classic fable "The Man, the Boy, and the Donkey." A man and his son were going to the market with their donkey. Someone mocked them for walking instead of riding, so the boy climbed up and rode on the donkey. Then a group of men criticized the boy for riding while the father walked, so they switched places. Next a couple of women shook their heads at the father because he was making his poor boy walk, so they both rode the donkey. Finally, after other townspeople were upset because they were overloading the donkey, the man and boy decided to carry the donkey between them. The poor animal struggled to get free and fell off a bridge into the river. The moral of the story? If you try to please all, you will please none.

If you're going to be a person who can handle criticism well, you need to learn the difference between good and bad criticism. Good criticism builds you up. That's why it's called "constructive." It might hurt like crazy, but it brings positive results in the long run. Bad criticism, on the other hand, is destructive. It undermines your confidence, it confuses you, it leads you astray, and it holds you back. Consider these differences between right and wrong kinds of criticism and see if you can identify which category describes the feedback you tend to listen to.

Bad Criticism	**Good Criticism**
Is vague and generalized "You're a bad person, a failure, a fraud."	**Is specific and detailed** "You did something wrong, but it doesn't define you."
Creates discouragement "This is just the way you are. You're hopeless."	**Creates hope** "You can change! This is doable."
Looks toward the past "You did all these things wrong."	**Looks toward the future** "You will do so many things right."
Focuses on blame "This problem is your fault."	**Focuses on responsibility** "This problem is in your power to change."
Finds reasons to condemn "This is why you're not enough and never will be."	**Finds reasons to believe** "This is why— and how— I know you can improve."

Think about the criticism and feedback you hear regularly. Maybe it's from a parent, a friend, a boss, or social media. Which category do their messages fit into? Are they providing healthy feedback designed to spur you toward improvement, or are they tearing you down by providing impossible standards and then mocking you when you fail? Do they see you for who you really are and motivate you to step into that reality, or are they shaming you and limiting you to some toxic snapshot they took of you during your worst moments?

Good criticism can be hard to hear, but ultimately, it brings life. But bad criticism leads to death. Whenever you're facing hard criticism, learn to look past the emotions and ego that arise. Determine if the message you're being given is for your good and should be accepted with gratitude and courage—or if it needs to be relegated to the spam folder of your heart.

You're Not Fighting a Bear

Once you've determined that a critique deserves to be considered, you're going to have to do some work inside your own head. Since criticism often feels like an attack, you'll need to disengage the natural defense mechanisms that kick in. Sometimes we're our own biggest enemies when it comes to listening to feedback that we really need.

Think back to the last time someone criticized you. What did they say, and how did it make you feel? Even if the person was gentle and kind, their words probably felt like a gut punch. They were bringing correction to something you said or did, and it's hard not to take that personally.

When you're attacked, your brain tends to react in one of several ways. I'm sure you're familiar with the classic fight-or-flight concept. While those two are common reactions to danger, there are a few others that get less airtime, including *freeze* and *fawn*. If you find yourself face-to-face with an angry mama bear in the woods, you'll try to defend yourself (fight), run away (flight), play dead (freeze), or appease her by offering her your lunch (fawn).

Realistically, most of us will go our entire lives without meeting an angry bear in the woods. I'm fine with that. Bear-fighting is not on my bucket list. But we can hardly go a day without meeting an angry person or at least an opinionated one. Everywhere we turn, we're met with criticism, comments, feedback, complaints, and "suggestions for improvement."

They feel like attacks. Sometimes they are, and sometimes they aren't. But what matters is how we perceive them because our perception determines our reaction.

Here's where this gets really practical and really personal. If you want to get the most from criticism, you need to know exactly how *you* tend to react so that you make sure your reactions aren't controlling your life.

When you are criticized, do you tend to fight? Is your first response to lash out and say, "Oh yeah? Well, you . . ."? If so, you need to make a conscious choice to lower your verbal fists and open your mental posture. Your harshness might "work" with some people, but it will mostly just silence those who really care about you and actually have something to say, like your family and friends.

Do you flee? Do you avoid conflict, avoid the conversation, avoid the person? If someone tells you something you need to hear, don't shut them out or shut them down. You need to listen to them, not run from them.

Do you freeze? Do you simply shut down and refuse to engage? Maybe their criticism triggers deep insecurity or shame, and instead of dealing with that, you simply shrink deeper into yourself. That's not helpful either, and it's not keeping you safe. It's just making you smaller.

Do you fawn? Do you try to people-please your way out of the conflict, even if the person is wrong? I think a lot of us struggle with this. While it's healthy to know how to get along with others, it's unhealthy to use "getting along with people" as an excuse to avoid necessary confrontations and hard conversations.

In and of themselves, these four things aren't bad. There are times you'll need to do them all. But the problem arises when they are reactions rather than actions. It's when your knee-jerk response to hard criticism is to fight, flee, freeze, or fawn.

Notice that none of these things deal with the actual criticism. They don't help you evaluate the person's comments and possibly make a change. They just temporarily deal with the conflict. They may help you end an awkward conversation, but at what cost?

I can answer that: at the cost of your growth. The criticism is there to help you, but if you view it as an attack, you'll react. You'll defend. You'll punch back, or you'll run and hide, or you'll shrink into a little ball, or you'll try to say the right thing just to make the person feel better. But you won't change—and change is the point.

Instead of getting defensive, get curious. It's just criticism, after all, not a bear. It doesn't weigh eight hundred pounds and have fur, claws, and fangs. The person is saying words. They are sharing ideas. They are making suggestions.

Lower your guard and listen. If you need to, take a few moments, take some deep breaths, and remind yourself that they are on your side or at least they're hopefully trying to be. Then lean into their observations. If you listen, you'll learn. You might not need to accept everything they say, but even wrong feedback can contain a grain of truth. Rather than focusing on the pain or on the person bringing the criticism, focus on what you can learn. Is there any truth to what's being said? That's what matters most.

Make a point of not taking things personally. This isn't about you as a person. It's about something you did or said, maybe, but that's not you. Too often we attach our identity and our value to every little thing, and if someone criticizes our performance, our opinion, our creative work, or anything else, we take it way too personally.

To counteract that, learn to separate yourself from what you do.

You are not your mistakes; you are a human who makes mistakes. That way you can objectively evaluate your performance in an area and make needed changes without going through a full-blown identity crisis.

Donkeys Make Good Points Too

When it comes to hard criticism, one error is so common it deserves particular mention: Often we discount what someone says by attacking them. We look at their character, motives, personality, or even tone of voice and say, "I'm not going to accept what they told me because they are so . . ."

The problem is they might be right. Even if you don't like them, even if they were mad when they spoke to you, even if they exaggerated a little bit, even if they have their own problems, they might still be someone you need to listen to.

I'm not talking about a peanut gallery critic here, but someone who is simply telling you something you don't want to hear. They are right or at least mostly right. They are making a valid point. But rather than listening to them, it's all too easy to write them off.

There's a Bible story that has always intrigued me about a man named Balaam, who was a prophet who spoke for God. He was hired by a foreign king to curse Israel, or at least try to, since he told the king clearly that he could only speak what God told him.

Halfway to the destination, Balaam's donkey (not to be confused with Aesop's donkey . . . that's a different story) saw an angel with a sword in front of him and swerved aside. She did this a few times until Balaam got so angry that he yelled at the donkey and hit it.

Then, unexpectedly, *the donkey talked back*, like some ancient biblical version of *Shrek*. They were carrying on a full conversation until finally God opened Balaam's eyes, and God told him that the donkey was smarter than he was because Balaam was trying to curse Israel for money.

My point is this: If God can use a donkey, he can use anyone. No, you don't have to please everyone or let the peanut gallery vote on every decision. But you do have to listen to the messengers God puts in your path.

Whom to Listen To

So how do you know whom to listen to? Whom do you relegate to the peanut gallery, and whom do you let into your heart? I find that it's all too easy to listen to the wrong voices and ignore the right ones. We try to please people whose opinions don't matter, but we don't take seriously enough the words of those who truly know us and care for us.

One way to know whether a critical comment is likely to be constructive or not is to look at the person who is criticizing you. Certain people deserve more of your attention and emotional bandwidth than others because they care about you and they are wise enough to give you good advice. Again, donkeys can make good points. But Balaam wasn't supposed to make the donkey his trusted adviser.

If we can learn to surround ourselves with people who will "speak the truth in love," as we saw when we talked about hard conversations, we set ourselves up for a lifetime of wins. How can you tell if someone fits into this category? Consider the following points.

First, notice their relationship with you. Are they close to you? Do they know you well? Have they proven they care about you? Have they walked in your shoes? Don't make the mistake of giving faceless online trolls the same level of access to your life as you would your close friends, family, and mentors.

Second, evaluate their level of knowledge and expertise. Do they know what they're talking about? Do they have education or other credentials? Do they have experience that could give them greater insight? Anyone can have an opinion, but what you really want are informed opinions.

Third, evaluate their motives as best as you can. Do they want to see you succeed? Do they love you? Do they believe in you? Or is there some selfish goal underlying their advice? Things like envy, greed, fear, insecurity, and offense can twist people's perspectives in ways they might not even recognize, and that will come out in their counsel and criticism.

Finally, consider their vision for you. Do they believe in your future? Do they let you change and grow? Do they see who you could be, not just who you've always been? If someone took a snapshot of you five years ago and never updated it, their criticism might be rooted in an old version of you. Listen the closest to people who let you be the best version of yourself.

Keep in mind, these are rules of thumb, not the Four Commandments for Dealing with Trolls. It's always possible a random, nasty comment on Instagram could be exactly the criticism you needed . . . but it's unlikely. In general, don't waste too much time or energy listening to opinionated people who don't fit into one or more of these four categories.

Of course, just because people check one of these boxes doesn't mean their criticism is right or their advice is helpful. We're talking about probabilities here. If they know you, have real wisdom and knowledge, want the best for you, and believe in you, listen to them carefully. Then decide what to do. You still have the final word.

Once you learn to take hard criticism well, you'll start looking for it. You'll ask for it. That's when your growth will really start to take off because you'll choose the voices you want to shape you. You'll invite them to share their opinions and counsel, and you'll be intentional about keeping your mind and heart open to change. It's a lot easier to take criticism when you're asking for it proactively, rather than when someone has to track you down and say, "We need to talk."

Whether you're letting an editor critique a book manuscript, a supervisor at work correct your performance, or a family member tell you exactly how you're getting on their nerves, don't overreact. Don't shut them out. Don't punch back. Find wise people who can speak into your life, then invite their honest feedback. On the other side of hard criticism, you'll find genuine growth.

Hard Criticism: Questions for Reflection

1. How do you usually respond to criticism: fight, flight, freeze, or fawn?
2. How could you get better at responding to criticism?
3. Is there an area of your life where you've recently received negative feedback? What truth is there (if any) in what they said? How could you improve in that area?

Getting Better Through Bumps

Write down a specific "hard criticism" you've been avoiding or resenting. What are the consequences of not addressing this? What are the benefits of addressing it? What practical step will you take *today* to embrace your hard criticism?

CHAPTER 11

HOLD ON, LET ME OVERTHINK THIS

(Hard Decisions)

I married my wife, Jen, the fifth time we saw each other in person. That's not something I'd normally recommend, and it certainly wasn't what we had planned—especially Jen. She had a dream wedding in mind, one that would have required a lot more time and organization. Instead, our wedding was a small affair, attended by close family and friends.

What caused us to change our plans? Jen is from Canada, and while the United States and Canada are on friendly terms, there are specific restrictions around marriage and visas that feel anything but friendly. Our immigration attorney informed us that if we got married in Canada, which was our plan, she would have to spend a year and a half there before she could move to the United States. That was crushing news. I couldn't leave my role in the United States for that long, and living apart for eighteen months was definitely not an option. So the attorney suggested we get married in the United States as soon as possible. Jen and I looked at each other, took a few deep breaths, and began rethinking everything.

The fact that we had seen each other in real life only a total of five times wasn't what made the decision hard. We were sure of our love, and we were confident in our relationship and commitment to each other. The hard part was setting aside our plans, dreams, and expectations in order to embrace a different future. We had to rethink, recalibrate, and reimagine. We had to evaluate the options and pick the one that was best in the long run, not the one that made us happiest or most comfortable or the one that fit our preconceived ideas of what "should" happen.

It was the right decision, and we knew God was in it. When the big day came, the wedding was perfect. It was beautiful, intimate, and unforgettable, and we wouldn't change anything.

Decisions are a part of daily life, and they are often hard to make. Sometimes they're difficult because they're urgent and the consequences could be serious. Other times they're difficult because you simply don't know what to do. Maybe you're frustrated with your job and wondering if you should look for a new one. Maybe you're dating someone and thinking about marriage. Maybe you're dealing with some health issues and your doctors are suggesting surgery, but you're just not sure.

Regardless of the nature of the decision you're facing, the point is this: Sooner or later, you have to make it. You must act. If you don't do anything, you're still making a choice—you're deciding not to decide, which will have consequences of its own.

The quality of your decisions over time will determine the quality of your life. Consistent good decisions lead to life; consistent bad decisions lead to hurt and even destruction. Proverbs describes this diverging path when it says:

> The path of the righteous is like the morning sun,
> shining ever brighter till the full light of day.
> But the way of the wicked is like deep darkness;
> they do not know what makes them stumble. (4:18–19)

I've said for years that we're born looking like our parents, but we die looking like our decisions. If you want to ensure that your life goes in the right direction for the rest of your days, pay attention to the choices you make every day. It's that simple.

On the bumpy road to better, decisions are like crossroads. They can send you left, right, or straight. They can change who you marry, where you live, what career you have, how much money you make, how much you enjoy your life, what you do with your talents and gifts, how you relate to your kids, whom you hang out with, what opportunities you get, and how you feel at the end of your life.

That's why you must be able to face hard decisions with wisdom and grace. Your ability to make the right choice at the right time is one of the greatest skills you can develop.

When you're faced with a difficult decision, how do you tend to react? Do you ask people for advice? Pray about it? Research and study your options? Think about it for a while? Freeze up? Make an impulse decision? Panic? Avoid it until you're forced to choose? Follow the crowd? Flip a coin? Make your best guess and go with it? At some point or another, you've probably tried all those things. I know I have.

How you make decisions will change based on the nature of the decision. Flipping a coin is fine if you're trying to choose an outfit in the morning, but it's a terrible idea if you're deciding whom to marry. The more important the decision, the more important it is to be wise and cautious in how you make it.

I can't give you seven foolproof steps to always make the right decision because those steps don't exist. Life is a lot messier than that, and you need to approach each decision on its own. However, there are a few things that are important in every decision, especially the hard ones.

Know Which Decisions Matter

This is something that is often overlooked: You must decide how much a particular decision matters. You might call this a pre-decision because it's a decision you make *about* the decision before you even *make* the decision. Essentially you're asking, "What are the consequences if I get this wrong?" Sometimes we forget this part, and it's one reason we can end up on a road we wish we hadn't taken.

For example, you might be the overthinking type. You tend to obsess over things that probably don't matter that much. As a result, you make good choices—but it takes you too long. You spend far too much energy trying to make every decision the best one, the right one, the perfect one.

If this describes you, I'm glad you take your decisions seriously. There are certainly situations where you should move slowly and evaluate every option. However, you have only so much headspace. If every choice is a life-or-death one in your eyes, you'll end up investing too much of your mental and emotional resources into the smaller decisions, and you won't have enough left for the big ones.

Rather than overthinking everything, start by considering how much this decision matters. Will this choice matter in six months? Are the consequences of making the wrong choice really that bad? What is the best that could happen? The worst that could happen? Questions like this override your brain's tendency to view every decision as life-altering and help bring things into an order of priority.

On the other hand, maybe you're not the overthinking type at all. Maybe you swing toward the opposite end of the spectrum. You make quick decisions, often based on intuition or emotion. You have a "figure it out as we go" mentality, even for larger decisions that affect a lot of people.

If this describes you, please know that your ability to make decisions is invaluable. There are many times when decisions simply need to be made, and you don't need to spend a week or a month or a decade thinking about them. However, intuition and emotion can also lead you astray, and for big decisions, you need to slow down and consider your options carefully through research, counsel, prayer, and reflection. This is particularly important if your decisions affect others.

Again, ask yourself: *What is the downside of getting this wrong?* In this instance, you *are* trying to scare yourself a little, but in a good way. If a bad decision would create pain and chaos for you and those around you, take extra time to avoid making a wrong choice. Don't rush into something you'll spend months or years regretting.

For both underthinkers and overthinkers, the point is the same: Be intentional about which choices you give more attention to. It's a simple step, but it brings clarity and balance.

Check in with God

Once you've determined a particular decision deserves extra attention, here's your second step: Check in with God. This one tends to get overlooked a lot too, but I've discovered that whenever I neglect to include God in my decisions, it's usually a guarantee that whatever I'm chasing will not be part of my future.

God wants to help you make the right decisions. We read in Psalms, "I will instruct you and teach you in the way you should go; I will counsel you with my loving eye on you" (32:8). Proverbs tells us, "Trust in the Lord with all your heart and lean not on your own understanding; in all your ways submit to him, and he will make your paths straight" (3:5–6). These passages and many others emphasize how involved God wants to be with the nitty-gritty details of our lives.

Checking in with God starts with prayer. James wrote, "If any of you lacks wisdom, you should ask God, who gives generously to all without finding fault, and it will be given to you" (1:5). If you don't know what to do, take time to pray about it. Open your heart to God's direction, creativity, and wisdom. He'll be faithful to lead and guide you.

This goes beyond prayer, though. It's about making sure your choice aligns with God's Word, will, and character. You aren't making this decision alone. Rather than doing what seems best to you in the moment, consider what God says is best. Proverbs 16:25 says, "There is a way that appears to be right, but in the end it leads to death." If we head into important decisions relying solely on our ideas, experiences, abilities, and knowledge, we're setting ourselves up for failure.

It's not that we're dumb or incapable. It's that life is far bigger than any of us. We can't see the future, much less control it. So when we're making crucial decisions, it's important to seek God's direction and ways.

Do you know which way God says is the best one? *Love.* The way of love is always the right way. Often we get ourselves into trouble by deciding based purely on self-focused motives: *What's in this for me? What's best for me? What do I want? What is easiest?*

That's not how God thinks, though, and it's not how he created us to live. Instead, in your decision-making, ask yourself, *What would love do here?* The Bible says, "Do everything in love" (1 Corinthians 16:14). When we follow that simple command, it's amazing how much clearer many decisions become.

Along with love, remember to go at the pace of *peace,* as we discussed earlier. Every decision made with God will be accompanied by his peace. The Bible says, "Let the peace of Christ rule in your hearts, since as members of one body you were called to peace" (Colossians 3:15). The term "rule" in this verse has the sense of arbitrating or deciding, like a referee at a sports event. God's command here is to let peace be a source of guidance.

Peace refers to the inner confirmation of the Holy Spirit that you are walking in the right direction. It's a connection point with God, and it's a place of faith and trust in him. For me, it's a feeling that extends beyond words, beyond emotions, and beyond logic. It's not that it's *contrary* to those things, but it's *bigger* than them. It comes from God.

Sometimes when you're going through a tough decision, your emotions and thoughts will be all over the place. Even amid storms and trials, follow the way of love and move at the pace of peace.

Focus on the Best Decision, Not the Ideal One

The third suggestion for making good decisions is to focus on picking the best option available *considering the circumstances*. Perfection is rarely an option, so keep your expectations as realistic as possible and work with what you have.

You might remember the story of pilot Captain Sully (Chesley Sullenberger). In January 2009, Sully was flying a commercial airliner with 155 passengers and crew out of New York when the plane struck a flock of birds, causing both engines to fail. With no power and rapidly losing altitude, Sully had to make an immediate decision: attempt to glide to an airport or make an emergency landing on the frigid Hudson River below. He chose the river. It was a daring and unprecedented decision, but he executed it with skill and precision. The plane landed intact, all passengers and crew members survived, and Sully became a national hero overnight.

The thing that stands out most to me is that there were no good options. Sully would have certainly preferred to have had at least one functional engine, but that wasn't the case. Rather than wasting time wishing for something he couldn't have, he made the best out of what he did have.

When you're stuck between a rock and a hard place, you have to relinquish your desire for the ideal solution. You can work only with what you have, so take stock of what exactly that is, show yourself compassion, evaluate the options—and then do your best. That's all any of us can really do.

Maybe your work is demanding too many hours, your family time is suffering, and something has to give. Or maybe you don't have the education and training you need to get the job you want, and you're frustrated at every turn. Don't just live in limbo, wishing for a magical solution that is cheap, easy, fast, and fun. Be realistic. Ask yourself, *What is the best option I have considering my limitations?*

Not every decision will be perfect, idyllic, and hassle-free. Most of them will be a lot messier than that. That's okay. The point is to make the most of whatever you've been given. If you lose one engine, both engines, or no engines, keep your head. Keep your cool. Work with whatever you have without judging yourself or getting angry at the world. Keep making the best decisions possible, and you'll have the best life possible.

Evaluate and Iterate

After you've made your decision and begun to act on it, there's one more step: reflecting and learning from your choice. Life is a series of experiments, and each one should move you further along. We talked about this trial-and-error process when we were looking at "hard consequences." Evaluation isn't about beating yourself up over a bad decision or second-guessing every choice you make. Instead, it's about doing what God designed you to do: grow. An unevaluated decision—even a good one—is a missed opportunity for growth.

Once a little bit of time has passed, take a good look at what you did and how it turned out. Be objective, and don't let shame or ego skew your evaluation. What went right? What went wrong? What could you have done differently? What surprised you? What are your takeaways? What should you tweak and improve? Where should you cut your losses and pivot to something new? What lessons will you file away for the future?

Often, the learning you gain from this process of reflection is more valuable than whatever benefit you received from the decision itself. Possibly you didn't make the best decision this time, but if you learned something that will shape you for decades to come, you're in a better place than you were before. Maybe your people skills improved. Maybe you learned how to invest money—or got better at spotting scams. Maybe you improved at conflict resolution. Maybe you learned not to hire people without a contract. Maybe you realized why putting gas in the car the night before is always a better choice than waiting until morning. It's time well spent to evaluate the outcome of your decisions, or you're likely to miss this invaluable benefit of the process.

Along with evaluation comes iteration. Most decisions aren't one-and-done situations that lock you into an inescapable set of consequences. Instead, they are steps in a certain direction, and those steps can (and must) be redirected as you move along the path of life. Maybe a decision you made today wasn't the greatest, but that doesn't mean you can't get creative about improving your situation tomorrow. Don't wallow in shame or insecurity; get curious. Get experimental. Take notes, make changes, and try again.

Sometimes we put too much pressure on ourselves to get every decision right the first time. We should get as many of them right as we can, especially the important ones—and we should get them as right as possible (which will never be perfect in this imperfect world). But at the end of the day, most decisions are a work in progress. We don't just *have* to live with our choices, as people often say; rather, we *get* to live with them, and we get to keep improving them. The Bible says that God's "mercies begin afresh each morning" (Lamentations 3:23 NLT). I love the idea that every morning is a fresh chance to reflect and grow into the people God has created us to be.

So much of life comes down to managing your decision-making under pressure—not just once, not just for a few months, but over the course of a lifetime. Thankfully, most of the decisions won't be as dramatic as landing an airliner on a river or getting married the fifth time you see your significant other in person, but they'll have life-altering effects just the same.

Know which decisions matter. Check in with God. Then focus on making the best decision you can under the circumstances. Over time, your life will become the reflection of that consistent wisdom, and you'll find yourself on a path that shines ever brighter.

Hard Decisions: Questions for Reflection

1. Think back to an important decision you made. Was it the right choice, considering the circumstances at the time? How did you make that decision? Would you do anything differently if you could go back in time?
2. In general, when you're facing tough decisions, how do you respond? What are your emotions? What practical steps do you take?
3. What is one major decision you are facing right now? Is there anyone you could go to and ask for advice or counsel?

GETTING BETTER THROUGH BUMPS

Write down a specific "hard decision" you've been avoiding or resenting. What are the consequences of not addressing this? What are the benefits of addressing it? What practical step will you take *today* to embrace your hard decision?

CHAPTER 12

THE UPSIDE OF DOWNTIME

(Hard Delays)

Have you ever sat in rush hour traffic and calculated how many human hours are being wasted? Don't do it. It's depressing. When you start multiplying the number of people around you by the minutes that everyone is sitting there breathing each other's exhaust, the number gets really high, really fast.

I don't know what you do in traffic jams, but I usually try a few things. First, I complain. This is my go-to strategy, and it's a terrible one. It doesn't help traffic move any faster, and it only makes my mood worse.

Second, I change lanes. "The traffic is moving faster in the other lane" is the urban equivalent of "the grass is always greener on the other side." This doesn't help either, and it tends to stress me out (and my wife, if she's with me) as well as make other drivers mad. Again, not a great strategy.

Third, I try to distract myself. I listen to music or a podcast. I think about a sermon I'm going to preach. I make a phone call. This is much better than the previous two strategies, but it doesn't take away the stress and pressure. It just pushes them to the edge of my brain for a while. Meanwhile, I'm still checking the clock and calculating how late I'm going to be for my next appointment.

Finally, once it's clear that things aren't going to improve anytime soon, I give up my need for control and simply allow the traffic to exist. I still don't enjoy it, but I embrace it. It is what it is. Traffic will move when it moves. I'll get there when I get there. Of the four, this is the only strategy that truly brings emotional relief because instead of fighting what I can't change, I accept it, and that frees up my mind to move past the delay.

This principle holds true in more serious delays. Maybe you imagined yourself getting married or having kids by a certain age, and it hasn't happened. Maybe you expected your career would have taken off by now. Maybe you were going to pursue a business idea, but life happened and you had to put it off indefinitely. In situations like these, it's easy to respond the same way I do in traffic: a mix of complaining, frantic efforts to get moving again, and killing time while you wait for the future you're convinced should be happening *right now*.

Delays of all sorts can be extremely frustrating. After all, we have things to do and places to go. Waiting is a waste of time.

Or is it?

Let's think about this for a moment. In our modern, urban, fast-paced world, we've been conditioned to think that efficiency is king. We must do more, be more, know more, see more, build more, buy more, play more. We have to wring every possible benefit from every single moment.

That's not even healthy, though. The fact that your body was physically designed to power down every night so you can lie there unconscious and immobile for multiple hours should be a daily reminder that you don't need to be moving all the time. Sometimes waiting can be good for the soul.

Embrace the Wait

Once you get past the initial frustration of unmet expectations, delays can have a deeply transformative effect on you. This happens once you "give up," in a sense. You're not giving up on your future, but you're giving up control of how (and when) you get there.

If you find yourself dealing with a hard delay right now, don't hate it. Embrace it. Look for the benefits hidden in your waiting. Let me share a few of the benefits of the "downtime" moments when you're stuck waiting for the fulfillment of a dream, plan, or project.

1. Delays let you practice for your future.

Earlier, we talked about the story of Joseph (Genesis 37–50). He's a prime example of someone who had to wait far longer than he expected for a dream that God placed on his heart. The dream wasn't wrong, but the timing of its fulfillment was meant to be later.

The delay wasn't pointless, though. While Joseph was waiting for God's vision to come to pass, he learned how to administrate Potiphar's business affairs, then he learned how to oversee an entire prison. It was a training ground for his future, when he would be Pharaoh's right-hand man, running all of Egypt.

The same principle is at work in your waiting. God is preparing you, shaping you, training you. You don't know the future, but God does. Choose to trust that today's delays are preparation for tomorrow's assignment.

This isn't wasted time. It's invested time. Rather than twiddling your thumbs waiting for "real life" to begin, focus on getting ready for what's ahead. Get more education and training. Read more books. Get experience wherever and however you can. Grow your skills. Build relationships. Take small steps that get you ready for larger ones later on.

When the time comes for your dream to be fulfilled, it might happen almost overnight. You need to be ready.

2. Delays build your character.

Whatever you build with your talents must be sustained with your character. God knows that. He can see the cracks and insecurities that are small now but may grow with pressure, and he often chooses to focus on those things first. That's a good thing. You have to be strong enough on the inside to carry the pressure and weight of success.

Delays have a way of revealing those cracks. They expose things like pride, obsession with control, greed, and wrong desires, which forces you to reassess your own motivations. As a result, you have an opportunity to grow internally, which is the best kind of growth.

It's easy for God to open doors for you, but will you be ready for it? Don't despise the waiting times. Instead, look inward. Let the Holy Spirit check your heart and make it more like God.

The list of character issues that God has worked on during my seasons of hard delays is long but precious. I can look back on business ventures, ministry goals, and relationships and see how seasons of delay drove me to God, and God did a deep, healing work that kept me from wrecking myself further down the line. Had success come more easily, I wouldn't be the person I am today.

Think about your own experience. What have you seen developed within you during times of waiting?

- Patience and perseverance
- Empathy and compassion
- Humility and putting others first
- Integrity
- Deeper relationships
- Better value systems
- Better thought patterns
- Faith, trust, and hope in God
- Wisdom, knowledge, and understanding
- Contentment
- Creativity
- Grit
- _____

These are some of the things God works into your heart and mind during seasons of waiting. Most of the time you aren't even aware of the growth any more than a child is aware of how his or her physical body is changing. But when you look back at who you were six months or six years ago, you're awestruck at what God has done.

3. Delays ground you in reality.

Every time you have to wait for something, it's a reminder of your own limitations. That's healthy. None of us are superheroes, and we really can't control all that much in our lives. Delays are a regular reminder that control is an illusion. We think we have things figured out, but life is complex and unpredictable, and we have to stay humble and connected to God, the only one truly capable of being in control.

I've found that delays are often a red flag that my expectations are out of line. I want things to be done faster than possible, or I don't take into account the inevitable hiccups along the way. Then I get bent out of shape when things take longer than I thought. That's on me, though. That's my problem. Rather than getting upset, I need to reevaluate my expectations.

The next time you find impatience or frustration rising, try reconnecting with reality and resetting your expectations. In this uncertain, often chaotic world, many things are simply going to take longer than you'd like. Build delays into your plans so that you're not surprised when they show up.

4. Delays give you perspective.

It's easy to rush headlong from one activity to another without stopping to evaluate where we are going and why we need to get there so quickly. We get caught up in the rush of our culture. Be famous! Be rich! Be powerful! Be seen! Be important! Be better than everyone else! Be king of the mountain!

But . . . why? Is that really what we want or need? Will it truly make us happy?

Delays force us to reevaluate what we want and why it's so important. And in so doing, they give us a wider and more long-term perspective. If we let God lead us, we start to discover simple truths like "money doesn't buy happiness" and "relationships matter most." If we had instant success in everything we put our hands to, we'd likely never question whether we are going down the best path, and we'd be worse off because of it.

It seems counterintuitive, but delays are a necessary part of moving toward our destiny. Rather than resenting them or raging against them, look for the upsides of the downtime. Let them train you, shape you, ground you, prepare you, and teach you. Your time will come, and when it does, this season of waiting will prove its worth.

There Is Joy Set Before You

Most of the time, delays come to us unannounced and uninvited—but we also need to *choose* to put off certain things to gain a greater reward later on. This is called *delayed gratification*, and it's an important ability to develop. Too often we sacrifice long-term gain for short-term pleasure, then we wonder why our lives aren't going the direction we wish they were. For example, if you choose not to eat junk food to achieve better health or if you sacrifice your free time to get a degree online, you're sacrificing immediate gratification for long-term rewards.

The Bible has a lot to say about living in a self-controlled, patient, wise way. For example, look at Proverbs 21:5: "The plans of the diligent lead to profit as surely as haste leads to poverty." Diligence has the idea of steadiness over time, whereas haste isn't able to handle the wait. While we all have urges and impulses, God gave us the capacity to control those and to choose a life based on intentionality and wisdom.

Jesus is the best example of this, of course. He had access to all the power and riches of heaven, yet he chose to live a humble life among humanity. He suffered, was falsely accused, and ultimately gave his life. The Bible makes it clear that in his flesh, he didn't want to die; but in his spirit, he knew he was taking the right path. That's why he was able to say to God, "Father, if you are willing, take this cup from me; yet not my will, but yours be done" (Luke 22:42).

You and I aren't being asked to go to the cross, but there are moments when we'll have to make real sacrifices today so we can reap greater benefits tomorrow. This is about self-control and self-discipline. It's about wisdom and integrity. It's about doing what we know is right, even when we're tempted to do something different.

If you want to be successful, you need to be able to delay pleasure. You can't give in to every craving, every temptation, every intrusive thought. Success requires discipline, and discipline means knowing the price you're paying now is worth the prize at the end. The Bible says:

> And let us run with perseverance the race marked out for us, fixing our eyes on Jesus, the pioneer and perfecter of faith. For the joy set before him he endured the cross, scorning its shame, and sat down at the right hand of the throne of God. Consider him who endured such opposition from sinners, so that you will not grow weary and lose heart. (Hebrews 12:1–3)

While Hebrews is talking about heaven, the principle applies to your day-to-day activities too. What is the joy set before you, and what do you have to endure to get there? Maybe it's following a diet, sticking to a budget, or getting to bed on time. Maybe it's staying pure in what you watch online to guard your mind and marriage. Maybe it's investing time into a relationship. Maybe it's going back to school and getting your master's degree. Maybe it's keeping your mouth shut instead of losing your temper when you really want to just tell someone off.

In the long run, it's not a sacrifice at all; it's an investment. You are delaying gratification or pleasure because you know that what lies ahead is worth it.

Your Times Are in His Hands

Ultimately, the ability to wait with grace is a reflection of your faith in God. Do you believe that he knows what you need when you need it? Or do you think you have to control your own fate?

David wrote this:

> But I trust in you, LORD;
> I say, "You are my God."
> My times are in your hands;
> deliver me from the hands of my enemies,
> from those who pursue me.
> (Psalm 31:14–15)

I love that phrase: "My times are in your hands." I should probably write it on a sticky note and post it on my steering wheel for those times I'm stuck in traffic.

Do you believe your schedule, your dreams, and your needs are secure in God's hands? Can you turn them over to him and allow his timing to be your timing and his ways to be your ways? If so, delays will be a lot easier, and you'll get a lot more out of them.

If you are experiencing any hard delays right now, whether they are ones you chose in order to pursue a higher goal or ones that were forced upon you, use that tension to propel yourself closer to God. Put your faith in him again, deeper than ever, and choose to trust him. Then let him speak to you about this season. He's with you every minute of every day, and he wants to help you get the most from it all—even the delays and downtimes.

Hard Delays: Questions for Reflection

1. How do you tend to react when you face a frustrating delay? Is there room for improvement there?
2. How have delays contributed to your personal growth? Look at the list on page X and write down any words that apply.
3. What delays are you dealing with right now? How are you handling them?

Getting Better Through Bumps

Write down a specific "hard delay" you've been avoiding or resenting. What are the consequences of not addressing this? What are the benefits of addressing it? What practical step will you take *today* to embrace your hard delay?

CHAPTER 13

WHAT DOESN'T KILL YOU MAKES YOU GO TO THERAPY

(Hard Healing)

I've always enjoyed sports and fitness, but a few years ago (okay, more than a few), I really got into working out. I even started taking a supplement called creatine to help with muscle gain and recovery. Between working out regularly and taking the creatine, the results were awesome. I was the biggest I'd ever been. I weighed 225 pounds and could bench-press 370.

One day, though, I felt a sharp pain in my side, like I'd been stabbed. Over the next three days, the pain got worse and worse, to the point that I thought my gallbladder or appendix was about to explode. I rushed to the emergency room. The doctor ran some blood tests, and when the results came back, he told me something was poisoning my kidneys and liver.

It didn't take long for him to figure out the culprit. The supplement I thought was so amazing was actually killing me. I had to have my liver flushed, and they put a tube in my side. And of course, I had to stop taking creatine immediately.

The cleansing process took a while, but eventually the pain went away and my levels returned to normal. Unfortunately, so did my muscle mass. Oh well.

That experience taught me the importance of doing whatever it takes to heal. In that case, I didn't have much of a choice. The pain was too bad for me to continue, and it drove me to find a solution. Of course, the solution wasn't what I would have chosen for myself. I wanted to look like Thor, but the price of that would have been pain and ultimately destruction.

In the same way, the pain in our lives is meant to motivate us toward healing. The reality is many of us would never seek healing if we weren't hurting. Life is too busy, our pride is too sneaky and stubborn, and our desire to maintain the status quo is too strong. Then pain comes along and stops us in our tracks.

It can be difficult to stop what we're doing, admit our need, and get help. But on the other side of hard healing, we find greater strength and deeper peace.

Pay Attention to Your Pain

Sometimes we refuse to listen to the pain. We think that if we can just tough this thing out, we'll get better on our own. So we sweep our pain, hurt, and trauma under the rug of misguided bravery.

You've probably heard the old phrase "What doesn't kill you makes you stronger." It's only partly true. Some hard things make you stronger because they develop perseverance and inner strength. But other hard things are supposed to motivate you to fix something that is causing actual harm, either to you or to others. You must be able to tell the difference between pain that is building strength and pain that is calling out for change.

What doesn't kill you makes you stronger *if and only if* you make the right changes and seek healing along the way. So let your pain motivate you to

- ask for help
- get advice from experts
- go to therapy
- manage your emotions better
- check in to rehab
- go to the doctor
- create a budget
- set healthy boundaries
- break up with an abusive partner
- deal with inner demons
- break destructive habits

That's just a partial list of how hard things can motivate you toward the healing your soul needs if you're willing to pay attention to the signs and symptoms. Sure, be tough and brave and responsible—but don't ignore alarm bells. Get help. Humble yourself and ask, seek, and knock until you discover the path toward healing. You don't win points for toughness if your toughness is really just pride in disguise.

God is on your side in this process. Psalm 147:3 says, "He heals the brokenhearted and binds up their wounds." God created your physical body to heal, and he created your inner self the same way. Both need some help at times, though, so don't just forge on alone, doing what you've always done and expecting the wound to magically disappear.

For me, the healing that needed to happen started when I listened to my pain. I had to seek professional help, change my lifestyle, and embrace the healing process. What is pain telling you? How are you limping from a past fall? Where are you bleeding from a past wound? How are you compensating for a trauma or a betrayal that never fully healed?

Healing starts by taking your pain seriously. It's telling you something, but you must listen to it. Only then can you address what is broken and begin your healing journey.

Fix What's Broken

Once you've determined that your pain is telling you something, the next step toward healing is to make sure you are not continuing to hurt yourself. Sometimes people skip this step, but if you don't deal with the pain at its source, any healing you achieve will be temporary.

Hebrews says, "Therefore, strengthen your feeble arms and weak knees. 'Make level paths for your feet,' so that the lame may not be disabled, but rather healed" (12:12–13). In other words, order your life in such a way that your current hurts can get better rather than continually being aggravated.

Is anything causing ongoing harm in your life? Identify it, then work on fixing it.

- Maybe it's a romantic relationship that is abusive or toxic.
- Maybe it's a work environment that is killing you or damaging your family.
- Maybe it's a bad habit or an addiction that has crossed a line.
- Maybe it's a friendship that is leading you in a direction you shouldn't go.
- Maybe it's a mental or emotional state that is spiraling out of control.

Whatever is hurting you, call it what it is. Stop making excuses for it, ignoring it, or minimizing it. You can't change until you admit what is broken.

It's crazy how easily and how often we defend the very things that are killing us. Maybe you've heard of Stockholm syndrome. It's when hostages or abuse victims develop positive feelings toward their captors or abusers over time and even begin defending them. It's not a good thing—it's a disorder, a trauma response. But we can do the same thing with certain parts of our lives that are holding us captive.

What are you defending that is holding you captive? Be willing to give up that habit, that relationship, that assumption, that offense. It's part of your story, but it doesn't get to tell your story. It's in your past, but it doesn't have to be in your future.

This doesn't mean you should cut everyone out of your life who causes pain, because that would lead to a very lonely life indeed. People are going to hurt you—even the good ones. But there's a difference between someone who hurts you as a normal part of messy human relationships and someone whose influence in your life is causing ongoing harm.

Proverbs says, "Walk with the wise and become wise, for a companion of fools suffers harm" (13:20). Paul wrote, "Do not be misled: 'Bad company corrupts good character'" (1 Corinthians 15:33). Take a look at your friend group. Are they helping you or hurting you?

Then ask yourself the same question about the rest of your world. Are your assumptions and mindsets helping or hurting? How about your habits? Your way of speaking? Your attitudes? Is there anything in your inner or outer world that is continually harming you?

That's half the battle right there: identifying the problem and setting your mind on finding a solution. Once you figure out the source of the pain, you're better able to stop the hurting and start the healing.

When the Pain Won't Stop

In this discussion of pain and healing, it's important to note that you can't always fix what is broken. Some pain is chronic pain. My wife has faced pain like this in her physical body for years, and I've seen firsthand how exhausting it can be.

There might be something in your life that is causing ongoing suffering, and you know it's not going to go away easily or maybe ever. Maybe it's a difficult relationship with a parent, a trauma from abuse in the past, a financial situation beyond your control, or a chronic illness.

The apostle Paul dealt with something like this. We don't know exactly what his tribulation was, but he wrote, "Three times I pleaded with the Lord to take it away from me. But he said to me, 'My grace is sufficient for you, for my power is made perfect in weakness.' Therefore I will boast all the more gladly about my weaknesses, so that Christ's power may rest on me" (2 Corinthians 12:8–9).

If you're dealing with a pain that won't go away—whether it's physical, mental, relational, or something else—the last thing I want to do is put a guilt trip on you for not being able to "fix" something beyond your control. You're a hero, and your inner strength is probably greater than anyone could ever know.

So what can you do when the pain won't stop? First, *accept the reality of your pain and make the most of the present*. You can still have hope and faith for the future, but don't live in the future—live in the present because it's all you have. Don't postpone life until you see a resolution. Live now. Enjoy now. Appreciate now. Even though you wouldn't have chosen to walk through the valley of the shadow of death, God is with you the whole way.

Second, *stay open to a miracle*. You never know what the future holds, so don't write off the possibility that your future could look much different than your present, if that is God's will. Maybe God will take this thing away, or maybe he'll give you strength in your weakness. Both are miracles.

And finally, *stay as healthy and healed as you can*. If something keeps hurting you, you're going to need to keep getting healed. Learn to protect yourself and heal yourself as effectively as possible. Find out what works for you. Is there anything you can do to reduce the pain? Maybe it won't go away, but can you make it more bearable? Can you recover from wounds more quickly?

If your pain is chronic and unyielding, I truly believe God's grace will be enough for you each day. And if your pain is due to something you have some control over, I believe his grace will help you make the needed changes, no matter how hard they are. Either way, once you've done what you can to keep additional wounds from occurring, it's time to start healing.

Embrace the Healing Process

If you're going to heal, you need to *embrace the process*. I say *embrace* because it's up to you to choose this option for yourself. Healing won't happen against your will. And I say *process* because healing rarely happens in an instant. You have to seek it, and you have to work at it.

I don't pretend to know how every hurt should be healed. Suffering is a tricky thing, and no two pains are alike. God is the great Healer, though. He told Israel, "I am the LORD, who heals you" (Exodus 15:26). Jesus spent a large part of his ministry healing all who came to him. He didn't focus just on their physical healing either, but he brought peace and life to their souls. If you open your heart and life to him, he'll be faithful to heal your brokenness and bind your wounds.

On your healing journey, here are a few things to keep in mind.

1. Speak from your scars, not your wounds.

When I'm communicating, I have an internal rule: Never speak from a wound. In other words, if an area of pain is too fresh, I don't talk about it publicly. Instead, I wait and I heal. I get counsel. I go to therapy. I give myself time and show myself compassion.

Once the wound has become a scar, then I can use the experience to help others. At that point, the pain is gone or at least diminished, and I can speak from who I truly am rather than from the pain of the moment.

If you're hurting right now, don't let your pain do all the talking. Give yourself time to heal before you make any decisions or pass any judgments, and don't try to rush to a place of superficial health. Not every question has to be answered immediately. Once you are strong again, things will make more sense, and you'll have more clarity.

2. Heal with other people.

You don't have to hide until you heal. As a matter of fact, you'll heal faster in community than in isolation. Surround yourself with people who can accompany you on your journey.

- People who know you and believe in you
- People who have been where you are now and have come out stronger
- People who are experts in the area you need healed: your body, mind, finances, marriage, etc.
- People who love you and are committed to you long-term
- People who will tell you the truth

This is one of the great benefits of having strong friendships, strong families, and strong communities. They are there when you need them. As we read earlier, in Ecclesiastes 4:9–10,

> Two are better than one,
> because they have a good return for their labor:
> If either of them falls down,
> one can help the other up.
> But pity anyone who falls
> and has no one to help them up.

We all need someone with what I call a "sidewalk perspective." They see us in ways we cannot see ourselves. They help us identify our blind spots. They warn us about potholes or dangers ahead. They help us believe in ourselves. They give us perspective, hope, counsel, accountability, and encouragement.

Just remember to *ask* for help! If you hide what's broken, nobody will be able to help you. Vulnerability is never easy, but if you're vulnerable with the right people, they'll play a key role in your healing.

3. Forgive and let go.

Sometimes forgiveness gets a bad rap because we don't understand what it is or what it's meant for. We use it to bury our feelings, gaslight our anger or grief, or silence other people. But forgiveness is not about denying the reality of what people have done. Rather, it's about finding healing from those things and moving forward in freedom.

Forgiveness is not a cover-up strategy; it's a healing strategy. Too often we treat it as something we can give or demand at will, but in reality, it's often a slow process of letting go. You have to release your desire for revenge, your bitterness, your need to fix things, your impulse to blame someone, your grief, your anger. That doesn't happen overnight. It's a choice—or rather a series of daily choices—to release yourself from the chains that hold you to the past.

Forgiveness doesn't change the one who hurt you; it changes you. While you can't choose what happens to you, you can choose your reaction to it. You can decide how long to let that thing affect you. If you don't forgive, something that was meant to hurt you once will hurt you for a lifetime because you'll continue to revisit it. You'll hold yourself hostage to a prison God never intended you to stay in.

Finally, *forgiveness doesn't mean you forget; it means you have the opportunity to forgive every time you remember.* There are people in my past whom I have to forgive all over again every time I think about them. That's okay. It's a way to practice the grace of God.

Forgiveness, like healing, is a process. Don't rush into it, but don't forget about it either. Make the choice to move toward forgiveness every day because each step, no matter how small, is moving you closer toward healing. On the other side of healing is freedom, life, peace, and joy.

What are your pain points? Where are you in need of healing? And what is the next step you need to take? Don't let stubbornness or pride hold you back. Make today the day you begin your healing journey.

Hard Healing: Questions for Reflection

1. Can you think of a time in the past when God took you through a healing process? How long did it take? What did you learn?
2. Is it easy or hard for you to ask for help when you need it? Why do you think that is? Do you think you could improve in this area?
3. Is there an area of your life where you need healing? What practical steps could you take to pursue that healing?

Getting Better Through Bumps

Write down a specific "hard healing" you've been avoiding or resenting. What are the consequences of not addressing this? What are the benefits of addressing it? What practical step will you take *today* to embrace your hard healing?

CHAPTER 14

PLAY THE LONG GAME

(Hard Losses)

It was January 14, 2023, and the Jacksonville Jaguars were facing the Los Angeles Chargers in the AFC Wild Card game. I was at the game, watching from behind the Jags' bench. The winner would go on to the playoffs; the loser would be done for the season. As the game progressed, the Jaguars' playoff dreams were being dashed to pieces one painful interception at a time. In the first half, due to a series of unfortunate events, they racked up four of them, along with a botched punt return that resulted in a fifth turnover. Shortly before halftime, the Jags were down 27–0. It wasn't just painful to watch—it was excruciating.

Over the season, the Jaguars had earned themselves the nickname "Cardiac Cats" for their tendency to be losing by a wide margin and then somehow come back and win games. But they'd never been down by this much before. Finally, the Jags put some points on the board with a touchdown a few seconds before the end of the first half, making the score 27–7.

At halftime, the commentators were using words like "nightmarish" to describe their situation, and the fans looked like they were ready to head for the parking lot. The Jags didn't give up, though. Both the players and the coaches doubled down on their resolve, and they spent halftime psyching each other up.

There's a recap of that Jags-Chargers game online that I've probably watched half a dozen times, and you can hear the players encouraging each other. At one point, wide receiver Marvin Jones Jr. said, "We've been in this position before. Just stop the bleeding. We're good. Let's just play our game. Let's just be us."[1] I remember watching another NFL video about the game, and Daniel Thomas, a safety for the Jags, kept telling his teammates: "It's a long game. It's a very long game. God gave me a dream that we're going to win, but it's a long game."

After the halftime break, they came out fighting for their lives, and momentum began to turn. They scored another touchdown halfway through the third quarter. The Chargers answered with a field goal, making the score 30–14. The Jags got another touchdown at the end of the third quarter, then a fourth one midway through the last quarter, making the score 30–28 with the Chargers still in the lead. A few minutes later, just as the clock reached 00:00, the Jaguars kicked a field goal to win the game 31–30. It was the greatest comeback in the Jaguars' history.

Even if you're not a football fan, you have to admire the fortitude and mental strength of a team that snatched a win from what seemed to be certain defeat. That line by Daniel Thomas—"It's a long game"—sums up their secret. They didn't let the first interception, the first quarter, or even the first half define them. They didn't let the scoreboard tell them what they could accomplish. They didn't listen to the voices of the commentators or the fans or their own self-doubt. Instead, they played the long game, and they walked away with the win.

Life is a long game—a very long game. God promises you a win, but you can't let momentary setbacks or hard losses take you out. You have to hang in there. You can't merely survive either; you have to believe and act as if momentum is going to shift and your comeback is right around the corner.

Too often, we let our current losses determine our long-term attitude. We make permanent decisions based on temporary discomfort, disappointment, or pain. That's not how God looks at our lives, though, and it's not how he wants us to see them either. On the bumpy road to better, we have to play the long game.

Wins Can Look Like Losses

In the game of life, you're going to have some wins, and you're going to have some losses. But remember, you won't always know what's a win or a loss *in the moment*. Unlike a sports game, there is no judges' panel or medal ceremony. Life is messier than that, and you'll go through some seasons and circumstances that feel like a loss for a while, but they're leading you to victory.

Don't be too quick to call hard circumstances a loss. They might feel like losses today, but life is a long game. Rather than assuming that defeat is inevitable, be ready for God's surprise ending. I'm sure you've read Romans 8:28: "And we know that in all things God works for the good of those who love him, who have been called according to his purpose." That means he takes what we think are losses and turns them into wins.

Can you think of a time this has happened for you? Maybe you lost a job, but then you got a much better one, and now you're glad you were fired even though it hurt like crazy. Maybe you didn't marry the girl or the guy of your dreams, and you're really glad today because you're living happily ever after with the spouse God had in mind all along.

Often, it's above our pay grade to figure out what is a win or a loss. Only God can see the end of the story, and his promise is that *it's all a win* for those who trust him.

The element of time is important here, as I'm sure you realize. That's why patience and perseverance are so important. They allow us to keep moving, to keep hoping, to keep trying, even when things take longer than we expect. When we do that, the situations we call losses often become our greatest victories.

I can't explain or control it, but I can testify to it. I've watched God take my limitations and mistakes and turn them into advances. I've seen him take what the enemy meant for evil and use it for good, as he did for Joseph. He's the God of the last minute, the king of surprise endings, the "Cardiac Christ" if you will. Just ask Mary, Peter, Thomas, or anyone else who got the shock of their lives when he showed up alive and well three days after his lifeless body was buried in a tomb.

His message to you today is "Don't give up!" You might be on the verge of a breakthrough right now. If you've still got breath in your body, let there be hope in your soul. God isn't limited by human scoreboards. He's not listening to the critics or the commentators. His eyes are on you for good, and he's leading you toward the victory he's planned for you since before you were born.

Remember, too, that losses can be disguised as wins. In other words, you can be tricked into pursuing something that appeals to your desire for ease, pleasure, or power only to find out later that you lost more than you gained. Jesus asked, "What good will it be for someone to gain the whole world, yet forfeit their soul?" (Matthew 16:26).

How do you avoid that? By keeping your eyes on Jesus, the "pioneer and perfecter" of your faith (Hebrews 12:2). If you walk in God's love, stay filled with the Holy Spirit, and imitate Jesus, you won't be deceived and distracted by the things of this world. You won't trade long-term wins for cheap trophies.

Take a moment to consider the things that feel like losses in your life right now. Don't judge yourself or condemn yourself, but let God show you how he sees those things. Can you find hope even in fear? Can you let faith rise in your heart? Can you trust God to work things together for your good, even if it takes a while?

Don't give up, my friend. Don't tap out. You might feel like you're so beaten up you can't continue, but it's only halftime. Jesus is your coach, and he's reminding you that if you just run the plays and stay close to him, you'll be okay. Losses will give way to wins, and you'll snatch victory from defeat.

True Faith Is Tenacious Faith

Earlier we looked at Hebrews 12:1–3, which speaks about this kind of resilience using another sports metaphor:

> Let us run with perseverance the race marked out for us, fixing our eyes on Jesus, the pioneer and perfecter of faith. For the joy set before him he endured the cross, scorning its shame, and sat down at the right hand of the throne of God. Consider him who endured such opposition from sinners, so that you will not grow weary and lose heart.

The writer pointed to the grit and determination of Jesus himself, who was willing to die to accomplish his goal. The word *perseverance* here is the Greek word *hypomone*, which means a "capacity to continue to bear up under difficult circumstances."[2] In contrast to patience, which is passive, *hypomone* is active. It fights back. It resists. It carries. It pursues. It finds a way forward. The author of Hebrews was saying that in this marathon called life, we need to keep moving even when things are difficult and we're tempted to quit.

This is tenacious faith, which really is the only kind of faith. Honestly, if our beliefs and convictions crumble at the first sign of resistance, we didn't have faith at all. We just felt strong emotions. Sometimes we confuse excitement with faith, but when tests and trials come, they reveal what is empty emotion and what is genuine confidence in God.

The good news is that not only do challenging circumstances reveal our faith, they also cause us to grow in our character. James wrote, "Consider it pure joy, my brothers and sisters, whenever you face trials of many kinds, because you know that the testing of your faith produces perseverance" (1:2–3). In this passage, "perseverance" is the same Greek word, *hypomone*.

Of course, "pure joy" is not an easy attitude to have when you're in the middle of a problem. I'm as guilty as anyone of wishing life would be easier and things would stop going wrong. In difficult moments, I've learned I have to take control of my own attitude and choose to lean into the difficulty, knowing that it will bring out the best in me.

Each difficult moment is a mentor, and each battle won is a lesson learned. When Marvin Jones Jr. was talking to his teammates during that Jags game, notice he said, "We've been in this position before." The team knew they could overcome a deficit because they had fought hard battles and won them in the past. I'm sure those games were difficult as well, but the team grew through them, and when they reached the playoffs, they were better because of how hard they had worked to get there.

Are you facing any hard losses right now? Maybe you're going through the loss of a relationship, a job, or a dream. Maybe you feel like one or more areas of your life are hopeless and defeat is just around the corner. Don't give up; grow up. Grow in strength, in courage, in humility, in patience, in creativity, in faith.

Every battle you face is a chance to grow in some way. You might not *win* them all, but you can *grow* in them all, and that's a win in itself. You'll discover who you are and who God is. You'll learn how to pray, how to adapt, how to grow. You'll find out how competent and creative you are with the Holy Spirit in your heart. You'll understand that the battle is the Lord's, and he's promised that you'll win at life as long as you don't lose heart and quit along the way.

One last quote from the game: Coach Doug Pederson told the Jags at halftime, "Guys, we just got to climb ourselves back into this game, one play at a time." One play at a time is *hypomone* in action. It's tenacious faith. It's stubborn courage. And it's what won the game.

Do you have tenacious faith? Do you have the ability to run the next play, then the next, then the next, no matter how far behind you are or how hopeless things seem? That's what is going to carry you to a win in life. You might not be the strongest or smartest person around. You might not have the resources someone else has. You might not have received the education or the opportunities or the easy wins. But can you persevere? If so, you're unstoppable.

Hard Losses: Questions for Reflection

1. Think about a time when something that seemed like a loss turned out to be a win in the long run. How did that experience shape your perspective on challenges?
2. What are some setbacks or hard losses you've experienced recently that have made you feel like giving up? How are you responding to them?
3. In what areas do you need to develop more tenacious faith, the kind that keeps going despite obstacles?

GETTING BETTER THROUGH BUMPS

Write down a specific "hard loss" you've been avoiding or resenting. What are the consequences of not addressing this issue? What are the benefits of addressing it? What practical step will you take *today* to embrace your hard loss?

CHAPTER 15

TIME AND CHANCE HAPPEN TO US ALL

(Hard Luck)

As part of my job, I spend a lot of time flying, so I've had my share of delayed and canceled flights. Recently, though, I had a trip that topped any flying experience I've ever had.

The backstory is that I had just flown home from a ministry trip to Africa, which was a thirty-two-hour journey. I landed early Sunday, then went to church and preached at the 9 a.m. and 11 a.m. services. From there, already exhausted, I rushed with my wife to the airport to catch a 2:30 p.m. flight because I had a wedding to officiate the following afternoon in Aspen for an incredible couple we love dearly. The plan was to have a night to recover, reconnect with my wife, and get ready for the following day's activities. What could possibly go wrong?

A hurricane, that's what. Hurricane Beryl chose that particular weekend to pound the Eastern coast. As a result, our flight was delayed three times, then finally canceled.

No problem—we were resilient and creative. We booked same-day flights on another airline through Dallas to Chicago because we were told we could fly from there to Aspen. However, when we arrived in Chicago at 1 a.m., we discovered that the flight we thought we could catch was canceled because Aspen's small local airport wouldn't receive flights after 10 p.m. That was fun news to hear in the wee hours of the morning when we were running on fumes and adrenaline.

We got about an hour's worth of sleep in Chicago, then flew back to Atlanta at 4 a.m. on yet another airline. We were getting desperate now because the wedding was scheduled to start at 4 p.m. PDT. Unfortunately, things didn't go any smoother. Our next attempt to fly to Aspen was also canceled. We were rebooked on a later flight, which was then delayed four times.

We finally took off at 2:11 p.m. CDT and touched down in Aspen at 3:32 local time, caught a taxi, and rolled up to the venue at 4 p.m. on the dot. The wedding coordinator was sweating bullets, and I'm sure I was more than a little wrinkled and frazzled, but we pulled it off.

I can't tell you how many times I thought during that long ordeal, *Why does everything go wrong? Can't we catch a break? We have the worst luck.* And just as many times, I had to talk myself back into a place of sanity and stability. *It's okay. Things happen. We'll figure this out. Oh, crap, they just announced another delay . . .*

In the grand scheme of things, ten delayed or canceled flights in one trip is more humorous than tragic. After all, we made it on time, and the couple in Aspen ended up married, which is what mattered most. But during the ordeal, the humor was hard to see, and we had to take turns talking each other out of some dark places. The human soul has only so much margin for bad news.

How much margin do you have for bad luck? Life is full of unexpected turns and surprises, and you'll experience some disappointing things from time to time. If you're going to navigate these hard-luck moments successfully, you'll need to grow in creativity and resilience.

Time Plus God Reveals All

You might be wondering, *If God is sovereign, does "luck" even exist?* Short answer: no, not really. God knows everything and rules over the entire universe, so he doesn't think in terms of good luck or bad luck. He's never surprised or shocked by a turn of events. God spoke through the prophet Isaiah:

> I am God, and there is no other;
> I am God, and there is none like me.
> I make known the end from the beginning,
> from ancient times, what is still to come.
> I say, "My purpose will stand,
> and I will do all that I please."
> (46:9–10)

God's foreknowledge and sovereignty should give you comfort and hope when you're going through dark times. You can't see what's coming, but he can, and you're safe in his arms.

Here's the thing: Although luck doesn't exist for God, it does for us, at least from our perspective. We know very little and control even less. Therefore, in our limited point of view, we experience a certain degree of luck or chance every day. Solomon put it this way:

> The race is not to the swift
> or the battle to the strong,
> nor does food come to the wise
> or wealth to the brilliant
> or favor to the learned;
> but time and chance happen to them all.
> Moreover, no one knows when their hour will come:
> As fish are caught in a cruel net,
> or birds are taken in a snare,
> so people are trapped by evil times
> that fall unexpectedly upon them.
> (Ecclesiastes 9:11–12)

Ecclesiastes is a famously pessimistic book, and Solomon was focusing strictly on the human experience without taking God into account. He was saying that, from a human standpoint, "time and chance happen" to us all.

As I said, from God's perspective, it's not chance. But we're not God, are we? If the term *luck* bothers you, think of it as "God's plans that he's not telling you about." I'm not going to argue the semantics of it, because my point is this: Things you don't expect will happen; they'll knock you sideways a little bit, and you must be able to adjust.

When I was staring forlornly at the long list of delayed flights, I certainly felt like the victim of bad luck, but I knew in my heart that God saw things differently. I had to hold both of those things at the same time: First, I was getting smacked upside the head with disappointment after disappointment; and second, God was still in control. It was valid to feel a little frustrated, but the story wasn't over, and I couldn't give up. All I could do was pivot and keep trying.

There's a time element involved here, of course, as we saw earlier when we talked about hard delays. Since you can't see the future, you might feel like everything is falling apart right now and nothing is working. You have to trust that eventually the broken pieces are going to come together—not like they were before, but in a new way, building a new reality.

Most of us aren't great at waiting, and we want God to make the discomfort go away right now. God honors time, though. He works within it. I've heard people say things like "Time reveals all" or "Only time will tell," which means that things will eventually make sense— but I don't think that's true. Sometimes time *conceals*, not reveals. I would say this: "Time plus *God* reveals all." In other words, you will grow in understanding eventually, and things will make more sense to you, but it's because God is going to reveal how he's been involved in your life from start to end. As you seek him and follow his leading, you'll find new doors, new paths, and new opportunities.

Be patient and hold on to your values even when things don't make a lot of sense. Don't make long-term decisions based on short-term feelings. Don't panic and do something dumb. Don't give up in frustration or fear. Don't sacrifice your integrity or your sanity out of fear of the future. Instead, keep your eyes on God, knowing that he is not the least bit shocked by the events that just sent you reeling.

From "Why Me?" to "What Next?"

Navigating hard luck is a learned skill. You can get better at this. Consider your own personality and habits for a moment. How do you respond when you get bad news? When things don't work out? When something breaks? When an accident happens? Are you good at this, or do you have some room to grow?

Bad news can be minor or major, slightly disappointing or genuinely terrifying, easy to adjust to or absolutely devastating. Maybe someone crashed into your car. Maybe you dropped your phone and broke the screen. Maybe your stock portfolio tanked. Maybe the market changed right when you launched a product. Maybe the used vehicle you bought turned out to be a lemon. Maybe you got passed over for a promotion. Maybe your finances have taken hit after hit through no fault of your own. Maybe you just received a terrible diagnosis from the doctor.

These "bad luck" moments hurt for a couple of reasons. First, because they are unexpected. They seem to come out of left field and at the worst possible time, and you feel shell-shocked because you were hoping for *good* luck and instead you got *bad* luck. Second, they hurt because they seem so unfair. You didn't choose this thing, and you didn't do anything to deserve it. Why did this have to happen to you? Why now? Why couldn't it have gone the other direction?

These internal "why" conversations don't help very much, because they are focused on the past, not the future. If you spend too long mired in self-pity, you can sink into a doom cycle of feeling bad for yourself, then feeling worse because you're feeling bad, then feeling even worse. Instead, switch up the question. While it's natural to spend some time picking up the pieces of your emotions, sooner or later you should transition from "Why me?" to "What next?"

Usually, only God can answer the "Why me?" question, and he's famously tight-lipped when it comes to explaining his actions. Remember the story of Job? He was wealthy, blessed, righteous, and happy. Then, through no fault of his own, he lost everything: his oxen, donkeys, camels, servants, and children. When you read the end of the story, you discover God was sovereign all along. But Job didn't have the end of the story to lean on. All he knew was that he was the victim of a series of extremely unfortunate events, and heaven wasn't giving him any answers.

James said this about Job: "As you know, we count as blessed those who have persevered. You have heard of Job's perseverance and have seen what the Lord finally brought about. The Lord is full of compassion and mercy" (5:11). Job lived thousands of years ago, but his story still shines as an example of navigating what must have felt like really bad luck.

The "What next?" question points forward, and forward is the only direction you can go. Rather than longing for the good old days, consider what you have in your hand right now and what lies ahead. Remember, just as we saw when we explored hard losses, whatever is affecting you now didn't surprise God, and that means he already has a plan for the future. He's giving you what you need to take the next step. He'll be with you all the way. He's going to open doors and show you opportunities you might not expect.

Think about your current circumstances. Are there areas where you've allowed "time and chance" to lock you into a reality that God wants to change? Have you resigned yourself to being a victim, a martyr, an unfortunate soul for whom life never seems to work out? Or are you continually taking stock of the resources at your disposal and asking yourself and God, *What's next? What can I do? What can I change? What can I learn? How can I grow? What doors are opening? What opportunities is God leading me toward?*

The Problem and Power of Expectations

Setting your focus on "What next?" doesn't deny the pain or frustration you're feeling, but it does help you not get lost in those emotions. There is always a next step. It may not be what you expected, but that's okay. Set aside your expectations and rethink your plan.

That's easier said than done, though, because we often don't take time to verbalize or criticize our own expectations. They are an invisible force that determines how we respond to the circumstances we encounter. When our expectations are met, we are pleased, and we feel like things are going well. When they are not met, we are disappointed, and we feel like we're the victims of bad luck.

The problem with unmet expectations is that they add to the pain of whatever we're experiencing. First, the bad news itself is painful. Second, our expectations are shattered. Both of those hurt.

For example, if you get let go from your job out of the blue, it's not just the fact that you were fired that hurts. It's the fact that you expected *not* to be fired. Now you're dealing with financial issues and a job hunt, but the process is complicated by the emotional aftermath of your violated expectations. You feel betrayed, hurt, confused, afraid, insecure, angry, and more. The sudden life change is hard enough, but the shattered expectation that you had of job security pushes the pain and shock levels even higher.

I've seen people more paralyzed by a broken expectation than by the event itself. Maybe their marriage fell apart, and since they didn't think that could ever happen to them, it left them bitter and withdrawn for years. Maybe their business failed, and because they were so sure it would succeed, they gave up on ever finding financial stability again. Maybe their health took a bad turn, and because they expected God to keep them healthy and pain-free forever, they sank into self-pity and anger. Their assumption of what would or should happen was so deeply ingrained that when it was violated, they couldn't recover.

Meanwhile, other people experience the same thing or even worse, but they bounce back. What's the difference? Often, it comes down to (a) whether they had the right expectations in the first place and (b) how quickly they are able to release unmet expectations and pivot in a new direction.

Again, though, we often overlook the presence and power of our sneaky, unspoken assumptions. For example, tomorrow I plan to have breakfast, drive to work, attend some meetings, write some emails, study for a message, drive home, spend time with my family, and go to bed. Built into all those planned events are dozens, maybe hundreds, of expectations. I expect to sleep well and wake up rested, to have eggs for breakfast, to drive through normal traffic, to have productive meetings, to send emails that are understood and acted upon, to make a lot of progress on my studying, to drive home at a reasonable speed, to have fun with my family, and to get to bed at a decent time.

Can you see how many opportunities there are in that simple list for me to be disappointed? I might sleep poorly, wake up late, not have time for anything but an apple for breakfast, get stuck in miserable traffic, have frustrating meetings, send emails that are ignored or misunderstood, get interrupted during my studies, have a flat tire on the way home, arrive to a grumpy family, and get to bed way too late.

I can choose to interpret all that as bad luck and throw an epic pity party for myself . . . or I can reset my expectations. It's my choice, and it's a choice that makes all the difference in how I experience my day. Often I want my luck to change, but it's my expectations that need to change. If I adjust what I assume life owes me, I can go from continually disappointed to constantly grateful. That's a much better way to do life.

Of course, it's healthy to have high expectations, so don't go to the opposite extreme and become an absolute cynic. Instead, strive to have right expectations, and then be willing to quickly relinquish those expectations if life deals you a different hand.

Is that easy? Unfortunately, no. It's hard enough to have that kind of perspective on a trip to Aspen during hurricane season, but it's even harder when the bad news has to do with your finances, family, health, or future. Give yourself grace and compassion, but keep learning and growing too. On the bumpy road to better, the ability to respond to hard luck with creativity, resilience, and trust in God is a skill you'll be glad you have.

Hard Luck: Questions for Reflection

1. Can you recall a time in your life when you felt like everything was going wrong? How did you respond to that situation, and what did you learn from it?
2. How does understanding God's sovereignty change how you view unexpected and difficult circumstances?
3. What are some practical ways you can cultivate resilience, creativity, and trust in God, especially when you're going through times where your expectations are not being met?

GETTING BETTER THROUGH BUMPS

Write down a specific "hard luck" situation you've been avoiding or resenting. What are the consequences of not addressing this issue? What are the benefits of addressing it? What practical step will you take *today* to embrace your hard luck?

CHAPTER 16

BRIDGES, BOXES, AND BOUNDARIES

(Hard People)

When I was six or seven years old, my family had a live-in nanny for about a year. Miss Laura (name changed to protect the not-so-innocent) was a terrible nanny and, quite frankly, a terrible person, at least to us.

She was also a good actress, though, and she had our parents convinced that she was a cross between Mary Poppins and Mother Teresa. Then, as soon as they'd leave the house, she would change completely. She would call us names and abuse us verbally nonstop, and I even remember her locking my sister in the closet for hours.

As kids, we didn't have words for what was happening. We just knew she was really mean, easily angered, and downright cruel. My parents finally found out what was going on when I asked them, "Would you ever call me a _____?" I filled in the blank with a word Miss Laura used when she was mad at us (which was all the time), and they freaked out. "Where did you hear that word?!" they asked me. So I told them. When they discovered who Miss Laura really was, they sent her packing immediately.

Eventually we got a new nanny, a genuine Mary Poppins/Mother Teresa woman. Miss Sandra was the most amazing caregiver, mentor, and friend we could ask for as children. She even became my godmother. Later in life, she was my assistant for sixteen years, until she passed a few years ago.

To this day, the difference between Miss Laura and Miss Sandra stands out in my mind as a clear illustration of people who harm us versus people who help us. I can easily look back and trace the *negative* effects of Miss Laura and the *positive* effects of Miss Sandra.

Now, Miss Sandra was no pushover. I remember her laying down rules, imposing consequences, and dealing firmly with our childish behavior. But we always knew her actions came from a place of love and genuine concern for us. When she said no, it was because she cared, not because she was cruel or cranky. When she made a decision, it was because she was thinking of our well-being, not her own convenience. Her underlying motivations and relational maturity made all the difference.

Do you have any Miss Lauras in your life? How about any Miss Sandras? Can you see the effects they have on you? Can you identify the negative or positive impacts their words and actions have had on your life?

I've heard it said that when God wants to bless you, he sends people into your life, and when the devil wants to curse you, he sends people into your life. In other words, people can be incredibly helpful and empowering, or they can be terrifyingly destructive. They are either the greatest blessing or the worst curse. They are your biggest source of joy or the reason you need years of therapy.

How do you deal with difficult, challenging, complicated, hard people? After all, most of the hard people you encounter can't just be sent packing like Miss Laura. A few of them are probably related to you. Some of them work with you. One or two might live next door to you. A couple of them are friends of yours, or say they are, anyway. Plus, a lot of people don't fit neatly into either of these two categories, which means you'll often find yourself dealing with some challenging behaviors or attitudes in otherwise nice people.

People are hard, but people are essential. You can't do life alone. Just think about how much of your childhood revolved around the people you were connected to: the parents or guardians who raised you, the siblings who surrounded you, the friends who influenced you, the teachers who shaped you. Then consider the power your relationships have today, including with your spouse, your kids, your friends, your extended family, your coworkers, your boss, your neighbors.

To an enormous degree, your interactions with the people around you determine the quality of your life. Your relationships have the power to bless you or curse you, to build you up or tear you down, to move you forward or hold you back.

That's why Proverbs 13:20 says, "Walk with the wise and become wise, for a companion of fools suffers harm." If you are surrounded by mean, cruel, selfish, immature people, they will affect you externally by inflicting harm on your life and internally by influencing your values and damaging your character.

Again, though, you can't necessarily remove hard people from your life. So what can you do? It's a question you'll wrestle with again and again. I've found that dealing with complicated individuals is one of the most challenging things in all of life. For that reason, improving my people skills has been—and continues to be—a top goal for me. I want to get better at discerning who is hurting me and who is helping me, and I want to know how to interface with as many kinds of people as possible—including the hard ones.

The Power of Connection

I've noticed that when I don't get along well with someone, my initial tendency is to blame *them*. I conclude the other person is too closed, too stubborn, too proud, too immature, or too *whatever*. I choose a label that makes me feel better about myself by shifting the blame to that person's deficiency. And of course, they're probably thinking about me in a similarly dismissive manner: I'm too busy, too distant, too demanding, too uncommunicative, and so on.

There's a glaring problem with this blame-based approach, though. If I look at the other person, I can usually find quite a few relationships in his or her life that are working just fine. And I know for a fact that I also have a lot of healthy relationships. That means neither of us are raving narcissists who are incapable of human connection. We simply aren't getting along. We aren't clicking. We aren't vibing. We aren't connecting.

The problem isn't *that* guy over there or *this* guy right here, but the broken bridge between us. Once I realize that, it's a lot easier to separate the conflict from the individual. I don't need to get defensive, nor do I need to go on the offensive. Instead, I can become more curious. I can take a closer look at what is coming between us. It's like the relationship is a third entity that needs to be treated as such.

I heard a relationship expert say that when he does marriage counseling, he often tells couples to get the biggest box they can find, such as the kind refrigerators are shipped in, and place it in their living room. The box represents their marriage connection, he tells them. Any time they have a conflict, they are supposed to go to the box and put something symbolic inside as a reminder that the issue isn't their spouse, but rather their relationship.[1]

Why such a large box? Because the relationship is its own thing, and it needs to be made visible and tangible rather than ignored. When most couples get in a fight, they completely skip over the connection piece and jump straight to blame-shifting and insults. Instead of working on the box, they attack each other. That doesn't help anyone.

Of course, if you want to have a box for every wonky, prickly, quirky person in your life, you'll probably need to rob a refrigerator factory. I love his point, though. Instead of trying to "fix" the other person, fix your connection with them. Instead of making the issue personal by labeling and dismissing people, make it objective by examining your relationship.

Think for a moment about a difficult relationship you are dealing with. It might be at home, at work, at church, or somewhere else. What would happen if you stopped being defensive or offensive and instead became inquisitive? Try to think of some questions you could ask yourself (and maybe the other person) that could point the finger of blame away from the person and toward the broken connection. For example:

- What expectations do I have that I haven't communicated?
- What assumptions am I making that need to be questioned?
- What is hard or complicated about me?
- How can I communicate better?
- What goals do we share? What goals are different?
- Am I bringing any baggage or past trauma into this connection?
- Am I holding on to offense, or have I chosen to forgive?
- Have I genuinely tried to see things from the other person's perspective?
- What is making our relationship hard, and what can I do about that?

Can you see how questions like these can help you reframe how you see someone else? The first step in any interpersonal conflict needs to be working on the connection between you both because that's a "thing" in itself. Once you're able to engage with the other person with empathy, understanding, humility, and compassion, you'll automatically build bridges instead of burning them.

Now, you probably won't turn a Miss Laura into a Miss Sandra just by tweaking your attitude or polishing your communication. People make their own choices, and some individuals are not going to be healthy. I truly believe those people are the exception, though. Many "hard people" are simply fallible, odd humans like you and me. With a little work and a lot of patience, we can strengthen the connections between us and turn a hard relationship into a healthy one.

How to Handle Hard People

Besides working on the connection rather than playing the blame game, what else can you do when you're dealing with challenging individuals? Let me give you a few suggestions.

1. Notice who is contributing to your purpose.

The Bible tells us to love everyone, but that doesn't mean you have to invite everyone over for dinner, go on vacation with them, or start a business with them. Some people simply aren't going to add anything to your life, and you aren't going to add anything to theirs. It's okay to recognize that. There is nothing wrong with keeping your list of close friends fairly small. Obviously you don't want to turn into a hermit, and be careful not to lock yourself into a clique, but you can open your heart and home only to so many people.

The litmus test for knowing whom to include in your inner circle is this: Does this relationship contribute toward each of you fulfilling your purpose? Are you helping each other become the people God created you to be and accomplish what he called you to do? If the answer is yes, then you are a gift from God to each other. If it's no, then try to stay on good terms with the person, but don't build your life around their opinions or let their values and goals determine your decisions.

There's an interesting story in Matthew 16 that shows Jesus exercising this kind of discernment. Jesus asked his disciples whom they thought he was. Peter responded, "You are the Messiah, the Son of the living God" (v. 16). Jesus congratulated him and told him that God had revealed that to him. It was one of Peter's shining moments.

A few verses later, though, when Jesus began talking about his imminent death, the Bible says that "Peter took him aside and began to rebuke him. 'Never, Lord!' he said. 'This shall never happen to you!'" (v. 22). Here, the reaction of Jesus was the complete opposite. "Jesus turned and said to Peter, 'Get behind me, Satan! You are a stumbling block to me; you do not have in mind the concerns of God, but merely human concerns'" (v. 23). I can only imagine Peter's embarrassment. He went from being so right to so wrong.

This story highlights the importance of discerning how other people are influencing us. Peter was on point sometimes, but other times . . . not so much. Jesus knew that if he was going to fulfill his purpose, he needed to listen to the right voices.

Notice this is a two-way street. Make sure you consider the people *you* are helping as well as those who are helping you. The closest, most empowering relationships are the ones in which you're walking together and building, encouraging, and protecting one another.

As you evaluate who is contributing to your purpose, keep in mind that even good relationships feel hard at times. This is especially true if the person is a mentor figure or a close friend who may need to tell you some hard truths. Some people are hard to get along with, but they're helping build your future. The discomfort they create is not toxic or selfish, but challenging.

This is what Proverbs is referring to when it reminds us: "As iron sharpens iron, so one person sharpens another" (27:17). Iron against iron will cause friction, heat, and sparks, but the result is a sharper, more effective edge. It's healthy to surround yourself with people who are willing to speak the *truth* to you in *love*. Both of those things are important. Your inner circle should be willing to tell you hard things, and they should be motivated by genuine concern for you.

2. Learn to be long-suffering.

While not everyone will be in your inner circle, you still need to do your best to get along with them. Paul wrote, "If it is possible, as far as it depends on you, live at peace with everyone" (Romans 12:18). In another letter, he said, "Be completely humble and gentle; be patient, bearing with one another in love" (Ephesians 4:2). This means patiently tolerating people's mistakes, lack of consideration, bad habits, and more. These people are hard to deal with, but they are still *people*, and God loves them. He expects you to do the same. You can love them on a spiritual level even if you don't enjoy being with them on a practical level.

The New King James Version of the Bible uses the word *longsuffering* to describe this attitude, and it is part of the fruit of the Spirit: "But the fruit of the Spirit is love, joy, peace, longsuffering, kindness, goodness, faithfulness, gentleness, self-control" (Galatians 5:22–23). The word is pretty much self-explanatory. It means having the capacity to suffer for a long time. If you are long-suffering, you can accept the humanity and fallibility of the people around you, which is an essential quality for healthy relationships because we all make mistakes.

This is about having appropriate grace for other people. God himself is long-suffering with us, and he wants us to show the same patience and humility toward our brothers and sisters. Yes, they're hard to deal with at times. But we are divinely equipped to do hard things.

Rather than letting people's meanness or lack of consideration drive you crazy, develop patience, love them sincerely, and let God deal with their character. You are responsible for your reaction, and a reaction of patience and long-suffering is usually the right choice.

3. Take the good, leave the bad.

The example of Peter speaking first for God and then for Satan within the span of a few verses illustrates an important point: Nobody is perfect, but most people have good things to say from time to time.

When you're dealing with hard people, try to learn from the good while rejecting the bad. Obviously if it's an abusive situation, you need to get out of it, as my parents did with our nanny. But assuming that's not the case and you're dealing with people who are just hard to get along with, try to focus on the things they bring to the table that can be of benefit. What experiences do they have that you've never had? What mistakes have they made that you can learn from? What knowledge and skills could they share? What perspectives do they offer?

Often we confuse "different" with "hard." We assume that because another's culture, personality, value system, age, or worldview is so different, any relationship is going to be more work than it's worth. But diversity is a *strength* if we learn to work together.

Rather than getting offended or trying to avoid challenging people, see if you can understand them better. There's a good chance they will be a blessing to your life if you're able to lower your defenses and increase your curiosity.

4. Set healthy boundaries.

Boundaries are limits that establish how you'll respond if other people act in certain ways. For example, if a coworker has been verbally abusive, you can let him know that if he continues, you'll report him. If a family member is toxic and creating harm to your family, you can decide not to let your kids go to her house until she changes her behavior.

Setting boundaries should be a last-ditch effort, after you've tried communication, patience, and understanding; otherwise, you're going to build more fences than bridges. If someone is hard to deal with, first try to connect with her, empathize with her, and reason with her. If she continues to cause harm, though, you might need to create some separation by establishing boundaries.

The goal here is to protect *yourself* from harmful influences, not to change the other person, because you can't change people anyway. All you can do is establish the consequences of their actions, then stand by your decision. Their response is up to them.

In some cases, the boundaries you set are internal. They are choices you make not to allow certain voices to influence you. I heard an African proverb once that says, "The lion does not turn around when the small dog barks." Don't allow yourself to be distracted from what you know is right by people or voices who don't have your best interest at heart. You don't have to believe every criticism or listen to every opinion, and you don't have to give everyone access to your sense of identity or self-worth. Sometimes you just need to limit the voices you listen to. That's a boundary, and it's yours to set.

These four things—notice who helps you fulfill your purpose, be long-suffering, take the good and leave the bad, and establish healthy boundaries—are by no means an exhaustive list, but they're a good start. Remember, your goal is to establish a connection with people, not change them or judge them.

When hard people come into your life, don't get mad. Get curious, then get to work figuring out how to relate better to them. There might be a Miss Laura or two that you'll have to wisely exclude from your life, but I believe the majority are sent by God to empower you and bless you.

Hard People: Questions for Reflection

1. How do you handle conflict with difficult people? Do you tend to become defensive, offensive, or inquisitive?
2. How do you discern whether someone is contributing to your purpose or hindering it?
3. What role do patience and long-suffering play in your relationships with challenging individuals?

Getting Better Through Bumps

Write down a specific "hard person" you've been avoiding or resenting. What are the consequences of not addressing this issue? What are the benefits of addressing it? What practical step will you take *today* to embrace hard people?

CHAPTER 17

OUCH

(Hard Questions)

Many years ago, I went through the process of divorce. That was a difficult time, as anyone who has experienced divorce can probably understand—full of hurt, confusion, and crushed expectations. I shared some of the story in my last book, *The Art of Overcoming*. After that experience, I honestly had no desire to get remarried. I didn't want to feel such deep pain ever again, and the idea of opening my heart to someone new was terrifying.

Thankfully, God had other plans. Eventually I met Jen, and she was incredible. Although she lived on the opposite side of the country from me, distance was not an obstacle for our romance. Things progressed quickly, faster than I could have imagined. Soon I was faced with deep, soul-level questions that demanded answers: Was I truly healed from my divorce? Could I be vulnerable and authentic? Was I ready to love again, to trust again, to risk again?

Those were hard questions, but they were the right questions. I couldn't skip them or rush through them. I had to find the answers deep within myself, with the help of the Holy Spirit. As I allowed God to examine my heart, I found comfort and assurance that I was healed enough and whole enough to receive love from the person I loved. The work I had put into healing had been effective, and I could reap the fruit of that inner restoration and growth.

When you come to a fork in the road, it's crucial to be able to ask the right questions. Often, those questions are not easy or comfortable, but they are necessary. If you don't ask these questions, or if you ask the *wrong* questions, the truth remains hidden. But if you put in the work of self-reflection and understanding, you begin to see clearly, and you can move forward with confidence and wisdom.

I wonder, how often do we miss out on healing and freedom because we don't ask enough questions or we don't ask the right questions? If we're going to stay the course on this bumpy road to better, we must learn to embrace doubt, curiosity, exploration, and change.

Need some examples? Try answering these:

- Am I truly happy, or am I settling for less?
- What am I avoiding in my life, and why?
- Am I proud of the person I'm becoming?
- What am I still carrying from my past that no longer serves me?
- How do I contribute to my own suffering?
- What resentment or unforgiveness do I need to release?
- How has my past trauma shaped who I am today?
- What would healing truly look like for me?
- What patterns do I keep repeating in my relationships, and why?
- What would I do differently if I weren't afraid of failure?
- What doubts do I have about my faith, and how do I deal with them?

Ouch, ouch, and more ouch.

Questions like these don't play easy. They get right to the heart of what makes us tick and what holds us back. I could list a hundred more questions—questions about God, about self, about trauma, about hidden sins and secret addictions, about habits, about relationships, about work, about dreams.

There are two complementary sides to question asking, and we're going to look at both. First, don't be afraid of *hard* questions. Second, ask the *right* questions. If you can master these two things, nothing will be able to keep you from fulfilling God's design for your life.

Don't Be Afraid of Hard Questions

Hard questions feel threatening because they make you evaluate your beliefs, your assumptions, and your behavior. They imply that you might be wrong about something, and that's painful for your ego to handle. They hint that a change might need to be made, and change is often scary.

Often, instead of questioning our assumptions or paying attention to our nagging doubts, we defend our version of reality. Somehow the status quo—even when it's less than ideal—can seem safer than changing our minds, learning something new, or making an adjustment in our lifestyles. We prefer to ignore the elephant in the room, even though the room is full of elephant poop and stinks to high heaven.

The problem, of course, is that we won't find healing and freedom as long as we're deceiving ourselves about what is real, true, and good. That's where hard questions come in. They break you out of complacency and toxic comfort and force you to move toward healing and freedom.

Hard questions come in a variety of colors and flavors, but here are two of the most important—and most difficult—categories to consider.

Questions About God

How do you handle doubts about God? I'm sure you've had a few. I have them regularly. One of the most common questions I get as a pastor is this: How can a good God allow bad things to happen? It's a hard question, which means it doesn't have an easy answer. Sometimes

God explains himself, and usually our perspective grows over time, but the fact remains that a degree of mystery surrounds God, and we need to be okay with that.

When I was growing up, I often heard my grandparents and others say, "Don't question God." They almost made it sound like asking anything even slightly negative about God was disrespectful or blasphemous, and lightning was going to fall from heaven and annihilate me on the spot. I don't think that way anymore. I'm fully convinced that God doesn't mind hard questions. All you have to do is read the Gospels to see how often Jesus answered his disciples' questions and addressed their doubts.

One story that stands out in my mind is of a father whose son was demon-possessed. The desperate man had gone to the disciples for help, but they couldn't cast out the demon. The father told Jesus that since his son's childhood, the demon had attempted to kill the boy by casting his body into fire and water.

Jesus said, "Everything is possible for one who believes" (Mark 9:23). The father immediately burst into tears and cried out: "I do believe; help me overcome my unbelief!" (v. 24).

I love that phrase because it describes my own walk with God. I believe . . . but I also doubt. I know God is able . . . but I wonder if he'll actually help *me*. I know God is faithful . . . but will he answer *my* prayer?

Jesus didn't rebuke the man for having a mix of faith and doubt. The man clearly wanted to have faith, but he also had to be honest about his questions. After all, think about what he had gone through for years on end. Who rescued the boy from the fire? Probably his dad, at least on some occasions. It's likely the man had scars on his arms and hands from saving his son. Similarly, who rescued him from the water? Who took him to doctors? Who took him to see Jesus? For years this man had lived with the reality that his son was ill. He had hope, but he also had scars. He had faith, but he also had doubts.

I do the same thing. When life is confusing, when prayers aren't answered quickly, when my expectations are unmet, when I feel powerless—it's hard to have a heart completely full of faith. The good news is that Jesus healed the boy despite his father's doubts, and that's what he does for us too. God doesn't ask for perfect faith; he asks for honest faith—growing faith, question-asking faith.

I find it interesting that, later, the disciples asked Jesus why they couldn't cast out the demon, and Jesus told them that kind would come out only by prayer. We often focus on that specific answer—prayer—but I think the point of this conversation is the *asking*. The disciples were smart enough to recognize their ignorance and humble enough to ask for help in a specific instance where they needed to grow.

Sometimes the answer to our questions is prayer, but other times it might be generosity, courage, action, or sitting down on our butts and just waiting. We won't know unless we ask, and we won't ask if we're scared of the answer. Faith isn't supposed to eliminate questions by reducing our spirituality to a series of memorized answers. Instead, it allows us to approach God with our questions in real time.

Honest questions don't deny our faith; they prove our faith. Why? Because asking for understanding is a key difference between doubt and unbelief. Someone who is in a state of unbelief has made a choice to believe a certain way. They aren't asking questions anymore because they've made up their minds: Life won't change, God won't help, their problems are hopeless.

If you have normal, human doubts, on the other hand, you are like the father in this story. You want to believe, but you need encouragement. You need direction. You need hope. So you take your questions to God in humility and honesty, and he is faithful to strengthen and direct you.

"God, where are you? Why am I suffering? What is the next step? What are you teaching me? How should I respond? What are you revealing about yourself? What can I learn right now?" Ultimately, questions like these grow your faith, even if you don't get all the answers right away. They point you to Jesus, and that's the best way to grow.

Questions About Yourself

The longer I walk with the Holy Spirit, the more I realize that his role is not just to reveal God to me, but also to reveal *me* to me. I have blind spots, bad habits, weird beliefs, wrong assumptions, hidden trauma, and more, and I need God to hold up a mirror and show me what needs to change.

Don't be afraid of asking yourself hard questions that lead to heart-level change. Questions like the ones I listed earlier will do exactly that. They'll help you peel back the curated, polished image you show the world and expose the intentions and thoughts of your heart.

This is a divine work, one you must participate in. David prayed:

> Search me, God, and know my heart;
> test me and know my anxious thoughts.
> See if there is any offensive way in me,
> and lead me in the way everlasting.
> (Psalm 139:23–24)

Like David did, allow God to help you question your heart, your thoughts, and your actions. Is that comfortable? Absolutely not. But it will save you a lot of grief and embarrassment in the long run.

When you become a question-asker, you keep two important truths at the forefront of your mind: *I have a lot to learn* and *I might be wrong.* In other words, you don't know everything, and even what you think you know might need to be updated or completely changed from time to time.

I meet too many people who are absolutely sure about what they believe. They know what the Bible means and how to apply it in every circumstance. They know which political party Jesus would vote for.

They know exactly how the end times are going to happen. They know how the economy should work. They know whom God loves and whom God rejects. They know what makes him happy and what makes him mad. They know what church should look like, how the pastor should preach, and what people need to hear. They know what everyone around them is doing wrong and precisely how they should fix it.

They might be partly right. But I can guarantee you they are at least partly wrong. We all are. We're all going to get to heaven and eat a slice of humble pie together because we all have some areas of ignorance. We all tend to blur God's purpose and our preference from time to time, claiming to have the truth when really we just have a tradition.

Sometimes I wonder what would have happened if Samson had started marketing donkey jawbones. Remember the story in Judges 15 where he killed a bunch of enemies with a jawbone? He could have claimed the power was in the tool and if people just bought his anointed jawbones, they'd have the same power. That's what a lot of people do today! But what works in one incident, season, or generation is not necessarily meant to work in another. We have to move with God. We have to keep learning, keep listening, keep experimenting, keep growing.

Questions won't keep you from making mistakes, but they'll keep you from arrogance. That is a gift that will carry you far.

Ask the Right Questions

The questions we ask determine the outcomes we receive. If we ask the wrong questions, we get the wrong conclusions, leading to wrong decisions, resulting in wrong outcomes. Novelist Ursula K. Le Guin put it this way: "There are no right answers to wrong questions."[1]

On the other hand, asking smart, pointed, honest questions goes a long way toward finding the answers you need. Framing your question is half the battle. Why? Because you can't solve a problem you can't describe or define, and asking questions forces you to put words to the issues. That's why therapists often spend most of the session asking questions rather than giving answers. If you can get the question right, the answer is often obvious.

Becoming a professional question-asker will make you essentially unstoppable because you'll never stop learning, so no obstacle will be too great. You'll either figure out how to overcome it or how to adjust to it, depending on the situation. If you face financial issues, you'll learn how to deal with them. If you go through health issues, you'll discover how to respond to them. If you experience tragedy or you are treated unfairly or you go through hard times, you'll never shut down your brain, which means you'll never shut yourself off from growth and progress.

Egyptian writer Naguib Mahfouz said, "You can tell whether a man is clever by his answers. You can tell whether a man is wise by his questions."[2] I love that. Clever is fun, but wise is far better. The wisest people I've met always tend to be those who have more questions than answers. They talk less and listen more. They stay curious and value learning. I love hanging out with people like that. They seem perpetually young because their minds are open, fresh, and interesting.

This doesn't happen by accident, though. You become a question-asker by choice, and you develop the art of question-asking through experience.

Take a second to think about your greatest challenge right now. Maybe it's an obstacle at your job. Maybe it's a problem with your marriage. Maybe it's financial debt you can't seem to overcome. Maybe there is a decision you need to make, but none of the options are good. Whatever it is, ask yourself: *What questions do I need to ask to get unstuck?*

Don't rush through this. If no questions come to mind, that's a red flag itself. Remember, this takes intentionality and practice, so don't expect it to be easy. Dig a little deeper. Think about whom you could ask for advice. Consider what class you could take, what book you could read, what topic you could study. Evaluate not just the options that are obvious but the ones that require thinking outside the box.

This is *work*, which is why people often don't do it. It's easier to look at the three or four options that are most obvious and pick the one that seems least likely to fail. But a great question-asker doesn't settle for the easy solutions.

Don't be in a hurry to fix things and move on. Keep digging. Keep exploring. Keep questioning your assumptions and expanding your mind.

When you do this, not only do you solve the problem at hand, but you grow in the process. I remember as a kid complaining about learning certain concepts in math. I said, "I'll never use these in real life." The answer from my teacher was "Maybe you will. Maybe you won't. But you're learning how to use logic and solve problems, and you'll use those things for the rest of your life." In the same way, each time you take a deep dive into the challenges you're facing and determine to find the best solutions rather than the easiest ones, you're teaching yourself to be a thinker, a problem-solver, and a learner.

I want to keep asking questions as long as I have breath in my lungs and thoughts sparking in my brain. I don't ever want to reach the point where I think everyone around me is ignorant and I have all the answers, or give up on finding solutions to a problem because the search is too much work, or settle for the status quo when help is just a question away.

Yes, some questions are hard. Some are awkward, some are intimidating, some are terrifying, some are vulnerable, some are confusing, and some are painful. That's okay. On the other side of hard questions are life-changing answers.

> ### Hard Questions: Questions for Reflection
>
> 1. Is there any long-standing pain or discomfort you have accepted as "normal"? What steps could you take to address this?
> 2. Do you tend to ask hard questions, or do you avoid them? Why? Do you need to improve in this area in any way?
> 3. What are some ways you could cultivate a mindset of curiosity, openness, and learning?
>
> **GETTING BETTER THROUGH BUMPS**
>
> Write down a specific "hard question" you've been avoiding or resenting. What are the consequences of not addressing this issue? What are the benefits of addressing it? What practical step will you take *today* to embrace your hard question?

CHAPTER 18

IT'S NOT YOU ... OR IS IT?

(Hard Rejections)

My heart was broken for the first time in sixth grade. I liked a certain girl, and she liked me. For a while, all we did was act awkward around each other and not talk about it. One day I mustered up the courage to do what you did back then, which was to write a note that asked, "Do you like me?" Underneath, there were three checkboxes: Yes, No, and Maybe.

I gave it to her friend because, again, that's just what you did. Then I watched as she unfolded the note while standing with a group of her friends. She read it, wrinkled her nose, said "Ew!" and tore up the letter.

And that, my friend, is how villains are created. I was devastated. Gutted. I avoided her like the plague that year, and I didn't talk to her at all until the next school year.

Life moves on, and each of us did too. I'm happy to say she married a great guy, and I married an incredible woman. But even though it's been thirty-odd years since she ripped my heart into more pieces than that note, I still haven't forgotten the feeling of being rejected.

Rejection sucks. Whether you were mocked for asking someone if she liked you, passed over for a job, excluded from a friend group, denied a membership, laughed at for a project proposal, turned down for a sale, or ghosted after a date, there's no easy way to deal with the pain. That person didn't just reject your romantic advances, ideas, or job application. They rejected *you*. Or at least that's how it feels. It's hard not to take rejection personally.

How do you typically react when you face rejection? Do you fight back? Shut down? Give up? Try harder? Pivot? Throw a tantrum? Get revenge? Laugh it off? Binge an entire TV series and a Costco-sized bag of chocolates in one evening?

My guess is that it's a combination of several of those. There is some grief involved in rejection, and as we saw earlier, grief has stages. If you've recently been rejected in an area you care deeply about, let yourself grieve. It's normal and healthy to take some time to process the death of a dream.

You can't live there forever, though. You need an exit strategy, a game plan to move forward. Hard rejections don't have to derail you; they can help you improve and advance if you handle them the right way. This starts by learning how not to take rejection personally.

It's Not About the *True* You

Rejection is usually going to feel personal because it's hard (maybe impossible) for us to fully isolate and disassociate from certain areas of our lives. We are holistic beings. When someone tells us no, when they snub us, or when they don't like our ideas, it's going to cut deep. I don't think we should ignore the fact that their rejection rocks us on a personal level.

But that doesn't mean we have to make their rejection part of our self-definition. It's one thing to feel normal sadness and pain because you were rejected, but it's another to extrapolate that rejection and make it a statement about your worth, your value, and your potential.

Sure, their rejection is about you in a sense, but it's not about the *true* you. It's only about your behavior, your words, your ideas, your performance, your weaknesses, your experience, or your mistakes. *But none of those things are the real you.* Not in God's eyes. They are how you show up in the world, but they are not the full picture of how God sees you, and they don't get to define you.

I've found that in order to be resilient in the face of rejection, I have to separate my true self from two voices that will always try to define me: other people's opinions and my own achievements. If I let them, these voices will push and pull me all over the place. They'll make me question my identity, my creativity, my sanity, and my significance.

First, think about *opinions*. The opinions of others are notoriously fickle. You can ask ten people what they think of you, and you'll get ten different answers. And if you ask those same people in three months, you'll probably get ten new answers. You can't tie the way you see yourself to the way others see you, and you can't determine your own value based on the value others see in you. That would be like tying a boat to one of those inflatable flamingo floats and thinking it's safely anchored.

God's opinion is the only safe, solid, secure thing you can attach your identity and worth to. That's what will hold you steady when rejection comes your way. You need to read the Bible and learn to see yourself the right way: as a child of God who is loved, known, seen, valued, wanted, capable, gifted, called, equipped, and empowered.

Second, *achievements* are just as fickle as opinions. You can succeed one day and fail the next. You can have success in three areas while messing up in three more at the same time. You can take three steps forward and two back, then two forward and three back, then one forward and four sideways, then . . . you get the idea. Don't try to prove your value or define your identity based on something that fluctuates as much as your performance.

One of the reasons rejection hurts is because it sabotages our sense of self-efficacy, which is our belief that we are able and capable to do what we need to do. The pain should be a reminder that we too easily connect our self-efficacy to our own abilities rather than remembering we are more than enough *in Christ*. If rejection knocks your legs out from under you, make sure you are standing on the rock of Jesus, not the sand of human achievement.

Jesus told his disciples, "I am the vine; you are the branches. If you remain in me and I in you, you will bear much fruit; apart from me you can do nothing" (John 15:5). Paul later wrote, "To this end I strenuously contend with all the energy Christ so powerfully works in me" (Colossians 1:29). These verses and many others remind us that we don't have to struggle through life alone, trying to prove our worth based on what we accomplish in our own strength. Our hope is in God, and he is actively at work in and through us, accomplishing *his* will with *his* power.

Rejection will come, and so will praise. At the end of the day, neither matters nearly as much as what God thinks about you. Learn not to be too devastated or too elevated by human opinion or personal accomplishments. Those things don't get to define the true you. Only God gets to do that.

Rejection Can't Hold You Back—Unless You Let It

God makes it clear in the Bible that we are infinitely valuable and perfectly planned. For example, listen to this poetic description from Psalm 139:13–18:

> For you created my inmost being;
> you knit me together in my mother's womb.
> I praise you because I am fearfully and wonderfully made;
> your works are wonderful,
> I know that full well.
> My frame was not hidden from you
> when I was made in the secret place,
> when I was woven together in the depths of the earth.
> Your eyes saw my unformed body;
> all the days ordained for me were written in your book

> before one of them came to be.
> How precious to me are your thoughts, God!
> How vast is the sum of them!
> Were I to count them,
> they would outnumber the grains of sand—
> when I awake, I am still with you.

Since God is the master Creator and the one calling the shots, it stands to reason that other people's rejection shouldn't be able to interfere with his calling on your life. We see this with Jesus. Peter told the crowd gathered at Pentecost, "Jesus is 'the stone you builders rejected, which has become the cornerstone'" (Acts 4:11).

Think about that for a second. Jesus faced frequent rejection throughout his ministry. On one occasion, he visited his hometown of Nazareth, and people were surprised to hear him teach. They were so taken aback that many of them rejected him. Mark wrote:

> "Where did this man get these things?" they asked. "What's this wisdom that has been given him? What are these remarkable miracles he is performing? Isn't this the carpenter? Isn't this Mary's son and the brother of James, Joseph, Judas and Simon? Aren't his sisters here with us?" And they took offense at him.
>
> Jesus said to them, "A prophet is not without honor except in his own town, among his relatives and in his own home." He could not do any miracles there, except lay his hands on a few sick people and heal them. He was amazed at their lack of faith. (6:2–6)

They could receive only from the Jesus they could see. Because their view of him was limited, their experience was limited. So Jesus had to move on and find people who didn't reject him or limit him.

Similarly, people who can't see who you really are will not be able to receive all the gifts that God has placed in you. That's not on you. That's on them. If Jesus faced rejection, don't you think you will too? And if he would shake it off and fulfill his destiny, can't you do the same?

Jesus was literally betrayed and crucified by the people he came to save—you don't get much more rejected than that. And yet, God's plan continued. The insults, betrayals, resistance, and lies of the people determined to stop Jesus accomplished nothing because God's plan was to use even those things to bring salvation to humanity.

Have you allowed human rejection to influence what you think God can do through you? If so, I encourage you to change your perspective because negative voices and opinions can't hold you back . . . *unless you let them.* If you believe the lies, you'll be limited by those lies. But if you let God's truth be your truth, no criticism or rejection can stop you.

Remember, those people can't see the real you. They have only a snapshot of you. Either they see who you are today, based on their experience, or like in Jesus' hometown, they have an outdated picture of you from the past, before you became the person you are today. Whichever it is, they are on the outside looking in.

God, on the other hand, knows your *future*, and he knows your *heart*. He sees you for who you truly are, and he calls you to walk in that fullness even if people around you aren't your fans. If people reject you based on superficial knowledge, that's their choice. But don't let their rejection discourage you from following God's plan. That is your choice.

Rejection Should Lead to Reflection

Rejection can't hinder your calling, but that doesn't mean it's useless and should be ignored. A wise person knows how to listen to criticism without being destroyed by it. This is where things can get tricky because you need a high level of emotional maturity to be both resilient and open at the same time.

For example, let's say you're passed over for a job, and you're feeling crushed. There are countless reasons this could happen that have nothing to do with you, of course. Maybe the company filled the role before they got to your résumé. Maybe the person who was hired had some sort of inside connection you don't have. Maybe the company was looking for something specific that you didn't have. Maybe they just flipped a coin.

While you can't allow yourself to feel responsible for a decision that is out of your hands, you can ask yourself if there is something you could learn for the next time. Could you make your résumé shorter or punchier? Could you be better prepared for the initial interview? Could you get some more experience, take a class, or get a certification? Could you carry yourself differently? Could you speak with more confidence, more humility, or more understanding?

Every rejection should lead to reflection, not to condemnation—that's something else entirely. When you hear a no, you should automatically go through a process of self-awareness to learn, change, and grow. Opportunities will come and go, and this won't be the last doorway you stand in front of. If you can learn from this closed door, you'll be better prepared for the next open one. That's all you can really do when a rejection is final: learn from it and move on.

Rejection Is Divine Redirection

Rejection should trigger reflection, but that's only the first step. Next, it should lead to *redirection*. This is where rejection gets redeemed because even though people told you no, their no is what enables God's yes. They closed the wrong door because God wants to open the right door. Their rejection did you a favor.

The way I see it, rejection occurs when God decides to upgrade you. You might consider it a tragedy and a loss, but that's not how God sees it at all. He's just eliminating mediocre options so you keep pursuing the best option, which is the path he's prepared for you all along.

Maybe that job you were passed over for seemed perfect because it paid six figures, but God knew it was going to kill you on the inside. It might have demanded all your time and energy, and your family would have paid a far greater price than the salary was worth.

You just don't know, but God does. When rejection happens, it doesn't usually come with a divine explanation. You simply have to trust that God's promises hold true, and he is actively, generously, and perfectly working all things together for your good.

When you look at it this way, rejection is a gift. It's a gift you love to hate, but it's still a gift. It's one of the many ways God guides and protects you.

You have to make this work for you, though, and that means getting up and getting back out there. If you choose to lie down and mope outside the closed door, you'll never find the open door. If you make the rejection your identity, you'll walk right past opportunity.

Remember, God's calling is greater than any rejection or criticism, so don't fall for the trap of victimhood or martyrdom. There is no endgame in those things. Yes, the rejection was hurtful; yes, it was probably unfair. But rejection is divine redirection. It's nothing but the backstory to your future victory. I know it feels like the entire plotline right now, but life is long and you are strong. Trust that God has a plan, then put yourself back out in the world. Date again. Love again. Create again. Sing again. Invent again. Write again. Serve again. Build again. Believe again.

Whether the rejection was a sixth-grade crush or a million-dollar career opportunity, you are more than someone else's no. God knows that, because he's the one who created you in the first place, before any rejection, criticism, or failure. Now he's pointing toward the open door in front of you and cheering you on. He knows your worth, sees your gifts, and values your calling. Do you?

Hard Rejections: Questions for Reflection

1. Can you think of any past rejections that had a lasting effect on you? Were you able to overcome them? How are you dealing with them now?
2. Do you tend to take rejection personally? How does what God says about you affect how you handle rejection?
3. Have you ever experienced a rejection that was actually redirection from God? How did you process that rejection? How have things worked out for you in the long run?

Getting Better Through Bumps

Write down a specific "hard rejection" you've been avoiding or resenting. What are the consequences of not addressing this issue? What are the benefits of addressing it? What practical step will you take *today* to embrace your hard rejection?

CHAPTER 19

YOU'RE NOT LOSING, YOU'RE CHOOSING

(Hard Sacrifices)

Aung San Suu Kyi is a Nobel Peace Prize–winning Burmese activist who has dedicated much of her life to promoting democracy and nonviolence in Myanmar (formerly Burma). As a result of her opposition to the military regime who refused to accept the vote of the people, she was placed on house arrest for a total of fifteen years between 1989 and 2010. She was separated from her children and husband for most of that time. Her husband developed terminal cancer in 1997, and even though she was not on house arrest at the time, she chose not to leave the country, fearing the military would block her from returning. The Myanmar government refused to grant him a visa. He died in 1999, and she was not able to visit him before he died.

In a 2010 interview, Aung San Suu Kyi said, "People ask me about what sacrifices I've made. I always answer: I've made no sacrifices, I've made choices."[1]

Let that sink in for a moment. Here's a woman who gave up her safety, her comfort, her freedom, and her family for a cause she believed in. And yet, her focus was not on *losing* something but on *choosing* something. She understood her own autonomy. She had the right to decide what to value, how to live, and what to pursue. She made peace with her loss by defining her win.

That attitude is inspiring to me because sometimes I lose sight of the win that lies ahead because I'm fixated on the loss that's staring me in the face. That fixation is a setup to fail, though. It's self-sabotage. I need to shift my focus from what I'm leaving to what I'm receiving.

Consider your life for a moment: your habits, your hobbies, your pursuits, your desires. Are there any sacrifices you need to make now so you can enjoy the future you truly want? Maybe you need to sacrifice some of your free time to accomplish a goal you've always wanted to reach. Maybe you need to quit a job that is taking you from your family. Maybe you need to give up smoking, alcohol, or another addiction. Maybe you need to give up some television time and carve out some gym time. Maybe you need to set aside your fear, pride, or insecurity and go to couples therapy so you can build a better marriage.

Now, in regard to those areas of sacrifice, ask yourself what you're focusing on: Is it the things you are losing or the things you are choosing? Have you made peace with your loss by defining your win, and are you pursuing that choice with courage and determination, day after day, in order to build the life you want?

You can set your eyes only on one thing at a time. Choose to focus on the future you want, then build that future by choosing the right things in the present—even when it requires some sacrifices.

Better Than Good

A few years ago, I was approached by a television network about doing a show. It was a great opportunity, and it would have given me a lot of influence for good. It also would have paid well—like, really well. It seemed to be an obvious open door, so I pursued the project. The pieces came together, and eventually we had a title, a pilot, and an air date.

I was feeling a growing unease, though. Then one day, God spoke to my heart. *Now is not the time for this.* The project was going to require a significant amount of my time and focus, and it was going to have a negative effect on what God has called me to do in this season, which is to pastor full-time. I made the decision to pull the plug. I set a meeting with a VP at the network and gave him the news.

The interesting thing is that I remember feeling much less emotional than I would have expected. You'd think that I would have been anguished, frustrated, and maybe even a little resentful. After all, I was sacrificing a significant opportunity to influence people on a national level (not to mention a good chunk of cash), all "just" to pastor the church.

I didn't resent it, though. I knew God had spoken to me, and the vision of his best was more than enough to remove any temptation to pursue second best.

In this instance, it wasn't about rejecting something horrible and doing something awesome. Both options—television show and pastoring—were good. But only one of them was God's choice for me.

Likewise, most hard sacrifices you make won't involve a choice between an obviously dumb decision and a clearly wonderful one. That kind of sacrifice would be a no-brainer and not really a sacrifice at all. True sacrifices are harder than that because the differences are more subtle. You have to give up something good in order to get something better.

I've realized that when God wants to elevate me, he usually eliminates something. Elevation requires elimination. Improvement follows investment. If I'm not willing to give up some *good* things, I'll miss out on some *God* things.

Following are a few examples of good things you might need to relinquish so you can pursue the better things that God has in store. Remember, nothing in the first column is wrong, so I'm not saying you should eliminate these things from your life. All I'm saying is to prayerfully consider whether any of them are keeping you from God's best.

Things you might give up:

- Time
- Money
- Immediate gratification
- Comfort
- Fame or reputation
- Leisure activities
- Sleep
- Convenience
- Hobbies or pastimes
- Certain relationships
- Short-term success or recognition

Things you might gain:

- Mental health
- Physical health
- Family unity
- Financial security
- Character growth
- Professional growth
- Personal fulfillment
- Long-term relationships
- Skills and knowledge
- Legacy and lasting impact
- Deeper faith and spiritual growth

Can you add to that list? If you identified any sacrifices you need to make, notice where they fit in those lists. Don't just identify what you're giving up, though. Pay a lot more attention to what you're gaining and where you're going. Imagine yourself receiving and enjoying those things. Let that vision of a better future replace your desire to hold on to a good (but less-than-the-best) present.

With the television show, the lesson I learned is that we need to make God's best our pursuit. If we don't, it's easy to justify nearly any "good" thing, and those good things will squeeze out the best things. The good thing will take up space, energy, time, money, or focus that should be invested elsewhere.

Only the Holy Spirit can help you know what that means for your life. For someone else, that show might have been God's best. It might still be in God's plans for me someday. That's up to him, and I'm okay with that. I'd rather follow his direction every day, striving to carry out his perfect plan, and let him direct my steps.

When you are asked to give up something good in order to follow God, it tests your faith and it reveals your heart. It helps you determine if your eyes are fixed on the gift or on the Giver.

That's the lesson Abraham learned when God asked him to sacrifice the miracle son he had promised him. Abraham was willing to obey, but at the last second, God stopped him and said, "Now I know that you fear God, because you have not withheld from me your son, your only son" (Genesis 22:12).

It's a strange story until you realize Abraham was fully convinced God would honor his promise, and Isaac would remain alive. That's why he told his servants when he and Isaac left, "We will worship and then we will come back to you" (v. 5). The author of Hebrews said, "Abraham reasoned that God could even raise the dead" (11:19). Abraham didn't feel like he had to disobey God to protect the good thing God had given him. He knew God was the source and, as James put it, "every good and perfect gift is from above, coming down from the Father of the heavenly lights" (1:17).

God isn't against good things. I believe he wants you to have money, health, fun, nice vacations, a safe place to live, possessions, and more. He's not out to take from you; he's out to give you more than you could imagine, "pressed down, shaken together and running over" (Luke 6:38). But if you want to receive those things without being distracted or destroyed by them, you need to keep your eyes on God. Otherwise, you'll be tempted to pursue those goals at the cost of other things that matter even more, such as your integrity, your peace, your relationships, your faith, and your walk with God.

Hard sacrifices are a reminder that life is about so much more than instant results or superficial pleasure. They keep your value system pure, your eyes focused on God, and your faith strong.

The apostle Paul knew what it meant to make sacrifices. He was in constant danger, he was in jail off and on for years, and ultimately he gave his life for the gospel. But he did it willingly because he knew the rewards of God's calling. He wrote:

> Therefore we do not lose heart. Though outwardly we are wasting away, yet inwardly we are being renewed day by day. For our light and momentary troubles are achieving for us an eternal glory that far outweighs them all. So we fix our eyes not on what is seen, but on what is unseen, since what is seen is temporary, but what is unseen is eternal. (2 Corinthians 4:16–18)

Paul was saying that what is seen might be good, but what is unseen is best because it's eternal and it's glorious. The passage reminds me of a quote by Jim Elliot, a missionary who was killed trying to preach the gospel in the jungles of Ecuador: "He is no fool who gives what he cannot keep to gain what he cannot lose."[2]

I'm not an apostle in danger of getting shipwrecked or thrown in jail, and I doubt I'll ever try to contact an unreached tribe in the jungles of South America, but I want to have the same value system Paul and Jim Elliot had. Whatever God calls me to is eternal and glorious, and whatever I leave behind is temporary.

Small Choices over a Long Time

Recently someone asked me what kind of sacrifices I make regularly, and my reply was rather embarrassing—especially compared to Aung San Suu Kyi and Jim Elliot. I answered, "Uh . . . well, my sacrifices usually have to do with food."

I love food. Dessert, in particular. Dessert is my favorite meal. Among my family and friends, my sweet tooth is legendary. It doesn't matter if it's cheesecake, red velvet cake, a cupcake, a donut, or a cookie, I will eat it, I will enjoy it, and I will want more. I am a true sugar connoisseur.

Unfortunately, I also come from a family with a history of high blood pressure, high cholesterol, and diabetes. Those things don't play well with unhinged sugar consumption, so I've had to make some lifestyle changes recently. One of those is to eat something sweet only once a week and strictly on the weekends. Usually it's a piece of cake on Saturday, in case you're curious. Also, if I'm eating at a restaurant and I could order an appetizer, a main dish, and a dessert, I'm saying no to two of those three things. Those are the rules I've been living by for some time, and it's giving good results. I've lost thirty-eight pounds in a year.

And yet . . . I still want cake. It's still a struggle to reach for the salad when sugar is sweetly calling my name. I don't know if it will ever not be a sacrifice to eat right, but it's a sacrifice I'm planning to make because I care about my long-term health, not just my short-term sugar craving.

Although cake is a relatively small sacrifice, the principle I want you to see is that often, sacrifice isn't an epic, one-time choice. Instead, it's about making small, right decisions over a long time. If you do that, the future will take care of itself. If you don't, you're locking yourself into a continuation of the present.

The good news is that anyone can make a small, right decision. While it can be overwhelming to think, *Crap, I have to do this the rest of my life*, you can choose to do it today, this week, and this month.

The key is to keep your focus on the *best thing* that you're reaching for rather than the good thing that you're setting aside. I can choose to stare longingly at the cake in the fridge, or I can choose to go enjoy my God-given health by playing ball with my son. It's up to me.

Each day, make right choices. It really is that simple. You'll probably make a few wrong choices along the way, but when that happens, self-correct. Don't wait until your health crashes, your finances implode, or your family falls apart. You have the power of choice, and every morning is a new day full of new opportunities to make right choices.

The Bible says, "Do not be deceived: God cannot be mocked. A man reaps what he sows. Whoever sows to please their flesh, from the flesh will reap destruction; whoever sows to please the Spirit, from the Spirit will reap eternal life" (Galatians 6:7–8). Sowing is an ongoing process. You keep doing the right thing, making the right choices, and following God's path. Those daily right choices—which sometimes feel like sacrifices—will produce a much greater reward.

It's important to note here that breaking an addiction is its own special breed of sacrifice. Not only do you have to make the right choice, but often you have to do so while your own brain and body are trying to force you to make the wrong choice. If that's your situation, please remember there is no shame in getting help. Rather than condemning yourself for failing and promising yourself you'll do better, reach out to someone who can assist you. We weren't meant to do life alone, and addiction is an enemy that is best defeated with a team around you. Of course, in order to do that, you might have to make a more subtle sacrifice: your pride. The ego inside us has a nasty way of keeping us from getting the help we need. If you're dealing with addiction, don't let embarrassment, fear, or pride convince you to stay silent. Make the right choice to get help today, then make that choice again tomorrow, and keep making it until you find the freedom you deserve.

Whether you're breaking an addiction, changing a habit, or simply navigating the complex choices of life, strive to make small, right decisions over a long period of time. You're not losing. You're choosing. And your future self will thank you.

Hard Sacrifices: Questions for Reflection

1. Reflect on a time in your life when you had to choose between something good and something better. How did you make that decision, and what were the outcomes?
2. What are some areas in your life where God might want to eliminate something in order to elevate you?
3. What small, right decisions are you making regularly that you know are building a better future? Are there other right decisions you should add to the list?

Getting Better Through Bumps

Write down a specific "hard sacrifice" you've been avoiding or resenting. What are the consequences of not addressing this issue? What are the benefits of addressing it? What practical step will you take *today* to embrace your hard sacrifice?

CHAPTER 20

THIS TOO SHALL PASS

(Hard Seasons)

My granddad was a sharecropper throughout my dad's childhood. Sharecropping at that time was basically a few steps removed from slavery. My grandparents and their eight kids all lived in a one-room tin shack, eating what they hunted and gathered. It was a hard, poverty-driven life.

Right after the birth of their last child, my grandmother began suffering severe health difficulties. Come to find out, a surgeon had left all the surgery gauze inside her body. It caused massive infections in her lungs and turned into a dire situation. The doctors had to perform major surgery on her and remove one full lung as well as half of the other.

After the surgery, she was on life support. The doctors said she wasn't going to make it, but they would give her a week, and then they would pull the plug. My granddad went into the hospital lobby and told God that if he spared my grandmother, he and his family would serve him. At the end of the week, the hospital took my grandmother off life support. God had answered my granddad's prayer—she recovered and went home, and she ended up living until she was ninety-two years old.

My granddad kept his promise by starting a little Baptist church in the community. It grew, and eventually he started a second one. He pastored both of them, along with sharecropping and holding a part-time job at the hospital. He became a well-respected figure in the community, and through his hard work, he was able to build a better life.

I remember hearing him tell his story, and when I asked him how he was able to keep going even when times were tough, he always said the same thing: "I just kept saying to myself, *This too shall pass*." It was one of his life mottos. He understood that seasons come and go, and you can't let yourself be too moved or shaken by any of them.

My granddad's perspective was that you can't assume the present will last forever. Pain feels eternal when you're in the middle of it, but just like it had a starting point, it will have an ending point. Because of his grit and tenacity even in the darkest of seasons, he was able to change his family's future for generations to come.

The question for you and me is this: Can we handle hard seasons with that kind of resilience? All of us will face some challenging times. We need a better plan than spiraling into depression, lashing out in anger, or simply giving up. We have to be prepared to face challenging times effectively with grit, courage, and wisdom. On the bumpy road to better, hard seasons can either knock you off your feet or build strength into your soul. It all depends on how you respond.

It Came to Pass

My granddad's motto has biblical origins. It's a transitional phrase that indicates things are changing. Something is ending and something else is beginning. One season is over and a new season has begun. A previous state of existence is giving way to something new. An event is about to happen that will shake things up in some way.

I think it's healthy to look at life through that lens. Things will come to pass—good things, bad things, unexpected things, happy things, tragic things, big things, little things, unfair things, confusing things, funny things, sad things, delightful things, painful things. Some will be predictable and maybe even controllable, but most are not.

Therefore, stop expecting life to conform to your idea of what it "should" be. If your goal is to create a perfect, beautiful, and fully controllable life, you're going to spend a lot of time frustrated because life doesn't behave like that. Instead, learn to roll with the punches. Plan as best as you can and try to stay in control wherever possible, but don't expect all your plans to succeed or get upset when things happen outside your control. Sometimes things just "come to pass," and you have to figure out what to do next.

In both hard times and happy times, I often remind myself, *This too shall pass*. The challenge I'm facing will turn into victory, and then in due time, the victory will be challenged, and then that challenge will turn into another victory, and then that victory will also be challenged . . . and the cycle will continue. I can't get so locked into my current circumstances that I forget the future will look as radically different from today as today looks from the past.

You might need to say to yourself right now: *This too shall pass*. If you're going through a tough, painful time, this phrase will give you hope and courage. As the Bible says, "Weeping may stay for the night, but rejoicing comes in the morning" (Psalm 30:5). Today's emotions don't determine tomorrow's reality.

On the other hand, if your life is awesome right now and things are going incredibly well, "this too shall pass" will help keep you grounded and humble. It reminds you that the future is not guaranteed, and you need to keep your eyes and hope fixed on God. It's interesting to me that the two verses that follow Psalm 30:5 say this:

> When I felt secure, I said,
> "I will never be shaken."
> LORD, when you favored me,
> you made my royal mountain stand firm;
> but when you hid your face,
> I was dismayed.
> (vv. 6–7)

In other words, when things were going well, David felt unshakable, immovable, invincible. But when God "hid his face," David realized just how flimsy and fallible he really was. In the New Testament, the apostle James reminded us of the same thing:

> Now listen, you who say, "Today or tomorrow we will go to this or that city, spend a year there, carry on business and make money." Why, you do not even know what will happen tomorrow. What is your life? You are a mist that appears for a little while and then vanishes. Instead, you ought to say, "If it is the Lord's will, we will live and do this or that."
> (4:13–15)

Of course, if you take this idea to the extreme, you'll never be able to fully embrace the present. That's not healthy either. "This too shall pass" is simply a reminder that life changes in an instant, not a doom-and-gloom prophecy that hangs over your head and keeps you from enjoying the blessings of God. It reminds you to make the most of today *while also* being prepared to pivot when unexpected things come to pass.

You Are Not Your Circumstances

Whether your life right now is terrible, awesome, or a bit of both, be careful not to let today's season become tomorrow's identity. Both pain and success have a way of taking more control of our emotions and thoughts than they should, but if we're going to navigate hard seasons successfully, we need to separate ourselves from our experiences.

Maybe you just filed for bankruptcy or your marriage ended or you were fired from your job. Those are difficult experiences—but they don't represent your identity. They don't define your worth. You mean far more to God than your financial picture or marital status, and you might need to fight to regain that sense of value if you've recently lost something that was artificially propping up your self-worth.

The ending of a season often highlights the unhealthy ways we attach our egos to our accomplishments. When the accomplishments are stripped away, we're forced to reevaluate what makes us important and valuable. That's a hard thing, but ultimately it's a good thing.

Consider just a few of the heroes in the Bible who were forced to find their value and put their faith in something greater than their circumstances or accomplishments.

- Sarah couldn't have children, despite God's promise to bless and multiply her and Abraham.
- Jacob had to flee his father's house, even though the birthright was his.
- Joseph was sold as a slave and later falsely imprisoned, despite his divine gifts and calling.
- Moses lost his position of power in the palace and fled to the wilderness, even though he was called to free Israel.
- David had to flee from Saul, despite killing Goliath and being anointed king.
- Job lost everything he had, even though he was a man of integrity.
- Mary watched Jesus die, even though God had promised her that her son was the Messiah.
- Paul was persecuted endlessly despite being called and gifted by God as an apostle.

These individuals and many more had to choose to find their hope in God, not in their own resources, connections, circumstances, or cleverness. Hard seasons of waiting and suffering proved their faith was real and their hope was solidly fixed on God.

Take a second to consider your own life. Are there areas where you've allowed your current circumstances to determine your sense of worth? Are you putting too much stock in either failure or success? Are you listening to voices that shout loudly but are soon going to fade into the past?

Life changes quickly, and you can't afford to let the season you are in define who you are. Only God can do that, so make sure you're keeping a distinction between your core identity and artificial sources of value such as what you own, where you work, or who comments on your Instagram posts.

You are loved by God, known by God, and called by God. That is what matters most, regardless of the season.

Time to Grieve and Room to Breathe

Hard seasons often bring a double whammy of pain. First, you lose something you valued or needed, such as financial stability or a relationship. Second, you enter a new season of hardship. While both are connected, they also represent individual pain points that you need to be aware of. Let's look at each briefly.

Loss

The last book I wrote dealt with grief, disappointment, and endings, and I originally planned to title it *The Funeral*. I thought the imagery of a funeral processional, eulogy, and recessional was a fitting metaphor. However, my publisher wisely told me most people won't buy a book with such a morbid name, so we came up with something more positive before we went to press: *The Art of Overcoming*.

Our aversion to funerals says a lot about the human reaction to loss and other "death experiences," doesn't it? It makes sense because these things hurt like crazy. So we pray and hope that bad things don't happen, and we hold on to our present happiness as fiercely as possible, and we buy books on overcoming rather than on dying ... and then one day, we find ourselves at metaphorical funerals, mourning the loss of things we once held dear. A business we poured ourselves into goes bankrupt. A friendship we cherished for years grows cold and distant. A career or job role we based our entire identity on disappears overnight. A position of influence is replaced with anonymity. A family relationship blows up and leaves us wounded and hurting.

Saying goodbye is part of life, and we need to stop pretending it isn't. The phrase "all good things must come to an end" has some truth to it. Times change. Life blooms and fades. Seasons come and go, and so does money and so do friends and so does happiness and so does health and so do cars and houses and clothes.

It's natural to experience grief for what you've lost. Don't rush through the mourning process, and don't condemn yourself for being "in your feels" for a time. You lost something, and that matters. You don't need to excuse it or explain it or defend it—just let it come, and find God in the midst of it.

For me, it's helpful to remember what are often called the "five stages of grief": denial, anger, bargaining, depression, and acceptance.[1] Although they don't necessarily happen in this order and you might not experience all of them, these emotions and reactions are frequently part of any hard transition. In times of loss, we might not recognize that the tumultuous feelings shaking our souls and minds are a subset of grief. Frustration, denial, blame-shifting, revenge, despair, and more are normal elements of mourning loss. C. S. Lewis is often quoted as saying, "I sat with my anger long enough until she told me her real name was grief." Instead of telling yourself just to stop feeling that way and instead of acting out based on emotion, sit with your feelings until you understand where they are coming from and what they are telling you.

Hardship

The second "whammy" is the challenge of adapting to a new and more difficult life. Not only did you lose something you miss—job, money, health, power, relationship—you must now create a new normal. Since change of any kind is usually uncomfortable, this process can be challenging and even frustrating.

Think of the pandemic that rocked our entire world not that long ago. Do you remember the confusing thoughts and emotions we all dealt with as we tried to navigate a world we knew would never be the same? Things felt scary, vulnerable, and sad. We suddenly realized how much we had taken for granted (like hugs and parties and toilet paper), and we wondered how we'd ever adjust. The world seemed to be crashing down around us.

Now, a few years out, we appear to have reached a new normal, one where sickness is taken more seriously, masks are more common, and Zoom meetings are a normal way of doing business. The pandemic is a bizarre, dark memory that feels like another life, even though it wasn't that long ago.

My point is this: Change often feels like the sky is falling and nothing will ever be right again—but it will be. It just takes time. In the meantime, though, you're going to experience a range of emotions. Feelings like resentment, fear, or anger for what you're being forced to endure are completely normal.

In these moments of painful transition, be intentional about giving yourself room to breathe, to think, and to grow. The temptation is to give in to fear and worry, but slow down and take the time you need to adjust to a new reality. You'll figure this out. You'll make a way. No, it's not easy, fun, or fair. No, you didn't ask for this or deserve it. But here you are. So what are you going to do? Panic and implode? Or adapt and grow?

Please don't take this as minimizing your pain, because that is the opposite of what I'm saying. Your suffering is real and valid. But pain doesn't get to tell your story. Only you and God get to do that, and he's actively working all things together for good. What feels like the end of your story is just the transition into the next season. The present might feel shaky, but the future is solid.

If you're going through a hard season right now, give yourself time to grieve and room to breathe. Don't ignore what you're feeling or suppress it or deny it or even judge it. But don't be overwhelmed by it either. You get to choose your reaction, so do whatever you need to do to work through the pain and loss and come out stronger on the other side. Go to therapy. Talk to friends. Read books. Take a vacation. Eat a piece of cake. Sing in the shower. Paint something.

This isn't the first time you've lost something you thought you couldn't live without, and it won't be the last. God is with you, and he's working all these endings and beginnings for your good. Whatever it takes, don't assume a hard *season* in your life is going to be the *story* of your life. In the words of my wise, resilient grandad: This too shall pass.

Hard Seasons: Questions for Reflection

1. Think about a time when you experienced a hard season in your life. How did it affect you emotionally, mentally, and spiritually? What did you learn?
2. How do you usually respond to difficult seasons? Do you think there are ways you could improve this response?
3. What does "this too shall pass" mean to you? Are there specific areas in your life where you need to remind yourself that the season you are in will not last forever? What are they?

Getting Better Through Bumps

Write down a specific "hard season" you've been avoiding or resenting. What are the consequences of not addressing this issue? What are the benefits of addressing it? What practical step will you take *today* to embrace your hard season?

CHAPTER 21

WAX ON, WAX OFF

(Hard Teachers)

I'll never forget when *Karate Kid III* came out in 1989. When I was a kid, we rarely went to the movies because there were seven of us in the family and finances were always tight, but I knew instantly this was something we had to see in the theater. I tried every trick in the book to convince my parents, with no success. They told me, "We'll just rent it when it comes out on VHS."

I was crushed. Back then, that meant waiting seven or eight months until it came out in our local Blockbuster, then fighting to get a copy. Meanwhile, all my friends saw the movie in theaters. They knew the plot, the characters, and the ending. I'm still dealing with bitterness, but God is healing me.

Those *Karate Kid* movies marked my childhood. The first one came out the year I was born, and by the time the third one finally hit Blockbuster, I *was* the Karate Kid. I'd wrap a dress belt around my waist and pretend it was a karate belt, and I'd practice the famous praying mantis kick until I was exhausted. I was convinced I knew karate.

Until I got into an old-fashioned schoolyard brawl and tried to use my karate moves. I discovered very quickly that I knew nothing about karate, and if I didn't abandon these moves and revert to street tactics immediately, I'd get my butt kicked. Forget fancy poses and precision kicks. I had to swing as fast as I could, protect myself, and hope to land a haymaker.

I learned a lesson that day: You are not who you *think* you are. You are who you *train* to be. I could dream and hope and dress up and kick the air all I wanted, but without lessons from a qualified karate teacher, it was all just play.

Ironically, in the first movie, the hero is a skinny kid named Daniel who has the same karate delusion I did, and he gets his butt kicked by local bullies. That's when a quiet, older man named Mr. Miyagi steps in and offers to train him. Mr. Miyagi is a hard teacher, and Daniel doesn't understand his methods at first. It all pays off at the end when Daniel faces his bullies in a championship and . . . I'm not going to spoil it for you, just in case your parents never took you to see it either.

Hard teachers are an essential part of your bumpy road to better. They help you go from just *thinking* you're good at something to *truly* being good at it. They take you out of the realm of dreams and hope, through the long journey of preparation, and into the reality of expertise.

Hard Teachers, Good Results

As we'll see in a moment, hard teachers can be actual people or they can be experiences that teach us something. Before we explore those two categories, though, let's think about the benefits of learning from these teachers. That's the goal, after all: to change, grow, improve, and expand as a result of the hard teachers God allows into our lives.

Consider Moses' complicated path to leadership. The first time he realized he was called to liberate his people from their Egyptian slave masters, he tried the praying mantis kick. Not really, but it was just as ineffective. He accomplished nothing except getting himself exiled from Egypt. He spent the next forty years in the wilderness, which must have felt frustrating, but turned out to be transformational. That's where he met God. It's where he met his wife too. It's where he dealt with his insecurities. It's where he received not just a calling but a strategy and a teammate, Aaron. Along the way, I'm sure he learned desert survival skills and leadership principles that were essential for his future. Those decades must have felt like a waste of time, but they were his preparation.

Similarly, when the people of Israel faced challenge after challenge in the desert, the events were meant to train and strengthen them. They were supposed to learn dependence on God, faith, obedience, and courage. God was preparing them for the battles ahead, and each miracle should have been fuel for their faith so they could eventually face greater challenges and experience greater victories. While the first generation ignored the lessons and failed the test, the second did not. They grew during their forty years in the wilderness, and when the time came, the school of the desert had prepared them for their victory in the promised land.

What are some things we learn from hard teachers? Here's a very partial list:

Skills

This is very specific to your situation, of course. What skills do you need, and who could teach them to you? Don't just think about your career either, although that's part of this. What talents and abilities could you learn that would help your family, your mental health, your physical health, and your spirituality?

Knowledge

Again, this is specific to your situation, so take some time to think about it. What you don't know often *can* hurt you, contrary to the popular phrase, so become a constant learner. Seek out people and other sources of information that will stretch your brain, expand your worldview, and address your blind spots.

Work Ethic

Everyone needs to expand his or her capacity to work, and hard teachers have a way of doing exactly that. You might hate the process, but the result will bring you rewards for the rest of your life.

Humility

Hard teachers help you see how far you still have to go. They don't let you think too highly of yourself or assume that you're somehow exempt from what everyone else is required to do. That's a hard lesson, but it's a necessary one. No matter how much you know, you will always have much more to learn.

Perseverance

Learning is rarely a quick, onetime event. Usually it's a process because you change on the inside before you can change on the outside. Because of that, you often find yourself under hard teachers *for a long time*, or at least for longer than you'd like to be. Rather than hating that, let it build resilience, patience, and perseverance. Learn to be tenacious in your pursuit of learning and growth.

Focus

When you learn hard lessons from hard teachers, it helps you eliminate things that are less important so you can focus on what matters most. Hard teachers—whether they are people or circumstances—force you to be practical and results-oriented.

Dependence on God

Hard teachers will often bring you to the end of yourself—in a good way. You'll come face-to-face with your weaknesses and limitations.

Rather than frustrating or discouraging you, this should point you to God. Ultimately, he is your source of success.

The desert was a hard teacher for the people of Israel, but God used the years they spent there to lead them into their destiny. They grew in faith, learned to obey God, and matured. Each lesson was further preparation to step into the promise.

In the same way, your hard teachers are part of God's preparation for your calling. He promises you a good future, but he needs to send some teachers to get you ready. If you can learn what you're meant to learn, you'll achieve what you're called to achieve.

Who Is Your Mr. Miyagi?

As I said, hard teachers show up in many ways, and many of them aren't literal people. If you look back at the chapters in this book, most of the hard things we've covered could be considered hard teachers: Battles, beginnings, changes, consequences, criticism, delays, losses, luck, people, rejections, sacrifices, and more will all teach you, if you're willing to learn.

Let's look at two essential kinds of hard teachers: the literal ones (mentors) and the figurative ones (experiences).

1. Mentors

These are real, tangible people with names, backstories, and personalities. They are individuals who motivate you to grow, change, learn, and excel. They might be a teacher at school, your parents, a sports coach, a boss, a therapist or life coach, or countless other influential mentor figures. Some of them might even teach you from a distance, via their books, videos, or example.

Individuals like this are a gift from God to shape your future. That doesn't make them perfect—they will have their share of defects that you have to deal with, overlook, or possibly even heal from. But the lessons they teach you through their words and actions are part of God's training program for you. The learning process is hard, but the lessons are worth it.

Of course, it's often hard to see the value of the teaching in the moment. In *The Karate Kid*, Mr. Miyagi made Daniel spend four days polishing cars, painting the house and fence, and sanding floors. By the end of it, Daniel felt that his time had been wasted. What he was doing was boring, difficult, and useless.

Then Mr. Miyagi threw a punch at him. The muscle memory Daniel had been developing for four days kicked in, and he blocked the punch. Mr. Miyagi wasn't just teaching him to wax cars. He was teaching him karate.

If you reject your mentors' wisdom, especially if it's because their methods are too hard, you're rejecting the reward on the other side of learning. Human nature is to look for shortcuts, not put in the work to achieve transformation. We tend to prefer our lessons quick, easy, comfortable, and cheap, but that's not how learning works, and you can't demand that people teach you according to your preference.

The Bible has a lot to say about listening to wise people and learning from them. For example:

- "Listen, my son, to your father's instruction and do not forsake your mother's teaching. They are a garland to grace your head and a chain to adorn your neck" (Proverbs 1:8–9).
- "The way of fools seems right to them, but the wise listen to advice" (Proverbs 12:15).
- "Whoever heeds life-giving correction will be at home among the wise" (Proverbs 15:31).
- "Apply your heart to instruction and your ears to words of knowledge" (Proverbs 23:12).
- "It is better to heed the rebuke of a wise person than to listen to the song of fools" (Ecclesiastes 7:5).

Notice the urgency and seriousness here. We are called to listen, not forsake, heed, and apply. Those are action words. God expects us to take wisdom seriously and put in the work for our own growth. We must take ownership in the process.

At the same time, passages like these are a reminder that God doesn't want us to just "figure it out" on our own. Sometimes we have the misguided notion that truly successful people are self-made. We assume they must be geniuses with an innate ability to figure things out and create their own futures. In reality, nobody is self-made because we all learn from others. If you look closely enough at a successful person, you'll find a supported person. You'll see someone who knew how to learn from and lean on the mentors they were blessed to have in their lives.

Do you value what someone else has? Maybe it's their financial ability, their family, their discipline, their strength, their creativity, or their entrepreneurship. If you want what they have, you need to learn how they achieved it. It's probably not as easy or quick as it appears from the outside, which means you need to humble yourself and allow them to impart the methods and principles *they* have found to be important.

Of course, sometimes your teachers don't have your best interests in mind, and a few of them will be problematic, toxic people. You shouldn't allow abuse to continue in the name of learning, which goes back to the boundaries we discussed earlier. But you can still learn a lot from difficult people: what not to do, what doesn't work, what hurts people, what undermines their future. Avoid these teachers if you can, but if you can't, be very selective and intentional about what you pick up from them. Don't learn their anger, their dishonesty, or their selfishness, but do glean anything positive you can along the way.

Life is full of teachers, if you pay attention. The hard ones are often the best ones, but you have to be resilient enough to let the lessons change you. Rather than avoiding challenging mentors, seek them out. Find people who will make you change, not make you comfortable. Look for teachers who stir you up, who call you out when you're wrong, who push your buttons because they see your potential, who believe in you more than you believe in yourself.

2. Experiences (aka trial and error)

While mentors are literal teachers, experiences are more metaphorical—but just as important. Julius Caesar once said, "Experience is the best teacher." (Actually he said "*Ut est rerum omnium magister usus,*" but luckily the phrase has been translated.)[1]

For example, you can sit in a class and listen to someone teach you the rules and theory of basketball, but you won't know how to play until you get your feet on the court and your hands on the ball. And even then you'll need a lot of practice before you can truly know how to play.

The same is true for most areas of life: Head knowledge is important, but hands-on knowledge is where you really grow and learn. Without experience, learning is theoretical. With experience, it becomes practical and transformational.

We were designed by God to learn constantly and in every situation. Learning from experience is nothing more than the infamous trial-and-error process, a time-honored part of being human. We talked about this earlier when we looked at hard decisions. From the moment we're born, we're trying out different muscles as we discover how to control our bodies and get what we want. That's how we learn to crawl, to walk, to climb stairs, to run, to ride a bike. Life is one long trial-and-error adventure.

In this adventure, it's important to value *experience* over perfection. If you're overly scared of failing, you won't try, so you won't learn. You have to overcome the fear of failure. Failure is your friend. Mistakes are healthy. In a society obsessed with perfection, being willing to fail is an act of rebellion.

Experience is valuable only if you learn from it, though. Leadership guru John Maxwell wrote, "Experience is not the best teacher.

Evaluated experience is."[2] If you make the same mistake eight times in a row, you're probably not reflecting, so you're not really learning.

Be willing to fail, and be willing to learn from failure. Neither of these is easy but both are essential. If you refuse to even try, or if you try but refuse to learn, then the trial-and-error process is going to become an error-and-error one.

This applies to anything you want to learn. Do you want to be a better parent? Do you want to be a better spouse? Do you want to be a better businessperson? Do you want to design a better product? Do you want to be a better friend? Do you want to have better mental health, a better body, greater influence, quicker results, more income, greater effectiveness at work, or more fun in life?

If so, come up with an idea and try it. Run an experiment. See what happens, analyze the results, make changes, then run another experiment. Did this activity you planned improve your family unity? Did this mental strategy create less anxiety by the end of the day? Did this way of communicating help resolve marital disagreements better? Did this money management create more stability? If it didn't, what went wrong and what could you change? If it did, how could you improve it even further?

You're not born knowing how to do anything. You try, fail, learn, adapt, try, and succeed, then do it all over again until you die. Get used to it. It's called being human, and it's wonderful, but you must make it work for you.

Remember, we're talking about *hard* teachers here, and learning by experience can be difficult. Go into this process with realistic expectations, patience, and humility. You'll embarrass yourself sometimes. You'll have to ask for help sometimes. You'll make expensive mistakes sometimes. The Bible says, "No discipline seems pleasant at the time, but painful. Later on, however, it produces a harvest of righteousness and peace for those who have been trained by it" (Hebrews 12:11). It's not always easy to learn from the hard teacher named "experience," but it's worth it.

Just like the Karate Kid had his Mr. Miyagi, God has teachers planned for you. Don't reject them when they come. Don't stop looking for them. And don't resent the challenges they represent. On the contrary, listen to them, learn from them, and grow because of them. On the other side of hard teachers, you'll find genuine transformation that leads to victory.

> ## Hard Teachers: Questions for Reflection
>
> 1. Think back over your life. What mentors have you had? How has each one shaped who you are today?
> 2. What "failures" in your life have ultimately led to personal growth? How good are you at embracing risk and failure as part of the learning process? How could you improve in this area?
> 3. What "hard teachers" are you learning from today? What criteria do you use to evaluate potential mentors?
>
> ### Getting Better Through Bumps
>
> Write down a specific "hard teacher" you've been avoiding or resenting. What are the consequences of not addressing this issue? What are the benefits of addressing it? What practical step will you take *today* to embrace your hard teacher?

CHAPTER 22

EASTBOUND ON THE SOUTH SIDE OF A MULE

(Hard Work)

My dad grew up working in fields owned by local farmers. The money he made didn't go to him; he had to help support the family, as was common back then. One of his jobs when he was maybe thirteen or fourteen years old was to till the ground before crops were planted. This involved following behind a donkey that was pulling a hand plow, guiding the instrument to plow straight lines.

It was hot, tedious, backbreaking work. But the worst part was the donkey had a bad habit of "breaking wind," as my dad put it. He would always say, "There I was, eastbound on the south side of a mule..." when suddenly he'd find himself dragged through a noxious cloud of gas, and he'd have to till a straight line anyway.

It was one of his least favorite jobs. Every day, he knew he had to do it, and every time, he barely lived through it. There was no reward, no payment—just a mule farting in his face. It was miserable.

He told me, though, that it did have a positive result. Besides the obvious fact that he was contributing to the family business, the hard work got him ready for baseball season. When the school year started, he didn't have to get back in shape. A flatulent mule and hard work had already taken care of that. He was ready to hit the baseball field running.

He also developed something even more valuable, something he didn't see at the time: a good work ethic. He learned diligence, responsibility, and discipline. He taught himself how to push through discomfort and get the job done. Those values and skills enabled him to make the most of opportunities for the rest of his life.

Proverbs says, "All hard work brings a profit, but mere talk leads only to poverty" (14:23). It's a simple principle that deserves to be tattooed on our brains. If something is worth having, it's worth working for. You can't just talk about or wish for it. You can't expect someone to give it to you. You can't pursue ease and comfort and expect it to magically appear. You have to work hard for it.

God created you to work. Sometimes people think work is part of the curse from Adam and Eve's sin, but work was around long before that. It's hardwired into humanity. The Bible says, "The LORD God took the man and put him in the Garden of Eden to work it and take care of it" (Genesis 2:15). That's part of the creation account. Sin later added a dimension of futility and frustration to work that wasn't there before, but that doesn't mean Adam wasn't working hard before the fall.

God wants humans to be involved in productive, creative work. We were made in God's image, after all, and he's a hard worker with an infinite capacity to build and create. It should come as no surprise, therefore, when our bumpy road to better includes a few farting mules along the way. Hard work is good, normal, and necessary.

The problem, though, is that we always seem to think we can find a shortcut.

Shortcuts Slow You Down

Have you ever thought you could beat the estimated arrival time on Google Maps or Apple Maps by taking a shortcut? Maybe the app said you were twenty-three minutes away from your destination, but you were sure you could shave a couple minutes off that. So you ignored the suggested route and took your own path, only to discover a few moments later that the estimated arrival time had jumped to twenty-five minutes. Maybe you tried a second shortcut, hoping to redeem yourself, and you lost a couple more minutes. Eventually, you probably gave up and followed Google's suggested route because it already calculated all the possible streets to take, and your "shortcuts" were only going to slow you down.

While efficiency is generally a good thing, our tendency to always crave better results with less time and effort can lead us astray in sneaky ways. Instead of putting in the work we need to put in, we take shortcuts that only slow us down. We chase easy money, easy fame, easy power, easy growth, easy success—and it turns out to be anything but easy. The Bible puts it this way: "The plans of the diligent lead to profit as surely as haste leads to poverty" (Proverbs 21:5).

When I was about sixteen, I remember a man who was selling a book and CD set about how to make money quickly. I think it was called *How to Make a Million Dollars in Thirty Days* or something like that. If I saw that title today, I would recognize it as a scam. Back then, I fell for it hook, line, and sinker. I was naive and eager for easy money, and that's a dangerous combination.

The worst part is that the set cost three hundred dollars. This was back in the late nineties, so three Benjamins for a sixteen-year-old was a fortune. But I figured it was a good investment. I worked hard and saved my money until I was finally able to buy this guy's get-rich-quick method.

Needless to say, thirty days later, I wasn't a millionaire. I was actually three hundred dollars further from being a millionaire. It was a terrible investment, and the memory still stings to this day. The only person making millions from that book was the author because he knew how to swindle idiots like me. I know what made me fall for his sales pitch, though: I wanted a quick, pain-free shortcut to wealth and success.

Another passage in Proverbs says, "Dishonest money dwindles away, but whoever gathers money little by little makes it grow" (13:11). While my goal wasn't to be dishonest, I didn't want the "little by little" approach. And yet, "little by little" is exactly what I needed. That's diligence. It's faithfulness. It's discipline. It's responsibility.

Are you willing to work hard and gather little by little? We're not talking just about money either. This is how you grow in influence. It's how you build a company. It's how you raise a family. It's how you create a strong marriage. It's how you develop genuine, lifelong friendships. It's how you establish your reputation. There are no shortcuts to truly valuable things. You have to work hard and grow little by little.

Of course, God will open doors of blessing you don't deserve. I'm not saying you will earn everything and deserve everything. Usually, though, those doors appear after a lot of hard work, not after sitting around and binge-watching multiple TV series. You ask, seek, and knock. You study and learn. You try new things. You gain wisdom and choose diligence. And somewhere along the line, God starts opening doors you don't deserve, and you're ready to walk through them.

God blesses faith, but faith without works is dead. Sometimes people say they're "waiting on God" when really God is waiting on them. They're confusing inactivity with faith. I've found that God will bless my feet when I walk in faith, and he'll bless my hands when I work in faith, but he won't bless my butt sitting on the couch. So don't waste time looking for shortcuts. Get to work, and little by little your blessings will accumulate and grow.

Private Diligence, Public Reward

People usually don't see all the hard work you put in over time, but they do see the rewards. They see your salary, your success, your family, or your career, and they say, "You're so lucky! Things are so easy for you." But they will never know how much time and effort you put in to get where you are.

I'm pointing this out because hard work is not very sexy, and it's often not fun. You shouldn't hate it, of course—hopefully you enjoy what you do and find fulfillment in it. But you'll probably experience quite a few moments where you're just sticking it out through sheer grit and commitment.

When you're in the middle of a long season of hard work, you have to think about the reward or you might give up. Someday you're going to see the results, and so will everyone else. But right now, you might be laboring in silence, eastbound on the south side of a mule, wondering if it's worth it.

- You might feel *left behind*, as if everyone else is somehow further ahead in life.
- You might feel *anonymous*, like nobody sees you or knows you.
- You might feel *useless*, wondering if your effort is futile and wasted.
- You might feel *discouraged* because it's taking longer than you expected.
- You might feel *exhausted* from the intensity of the labor.
- You might feel *bitter* because life seems to have betrayed you.

While I can't speak to the specifics of your situation, I can tell you that private diligence nearly always results in public reward. If you are faithful with little, God gives you much. If you are diligent in the shadows, God brings you into the light.

The story of Anna in Luke 2 illustrates this principle. Here's the entirety of what the Bible says about her:

> There was also a prophet, Anna, the daughter of Penuel, of the tribe of Asher. She was very old; she had lived with her husband seven years after her marriage, and then was a widow until she was eighty-four. She never left the temple but worshiped night and day, fasting and praying. Coming up to them at that very moment,

she gave thanks to God and spoke about the child to all who were looking forward to the redemption of Jerusalem. (vv. 36–38)

There is so much backstory packed into those three verses. Anna was widowed very young, probably in her early twenties. For six decades, she had been a prophetess and a worshipper in the temple. She knew the prophecies about a Messiah, and I'm sure she had dreamed of one day seeing God's promises come to pass.

Anna could have gotten bitter at God. She lost her husband, and she probably never had kids. Instead, she remained faithful—for sixty-plus years. As a result, she was in the right place at the right time. She became one of the first people to recognize who Jesus was, and she immediately went out and preached the good news. God trusted her to share the gospel to the people of Israel because she was diligent and faithful even when no one was watching.

The Bible says, "Let us not become weary in doing good, for at the proper time we will reap a harvest if we do not give up" (Galatians 6:9). If you feel discouraged or disappointed with how much work you've put in or how long it's taking to see results, take heart. God sees your faithfulness day in and day out. He sees your diligence in the secret place. Your reward will come in his time and in his way.

Easy Is Overrated

One of the main reasons we avoid hard work is because it's not easy. I know that seems obvious when you speak it, but it's important to acknowledge. Hard work is often inconvenient, unenjoyable, and boring. In a dopamine-driven society, work feels like the opposite of what we *want* to do.

Easy is overrated, though. That's true not just because we might not value things enough when they come too easily, but because hard work has value in itself. When you are forced to work hard, two things are usually happening simultaneously. First, you're moving closer to the reward of your labor. Second, you're being transformed on the inside. Both are valuable, but the second is more important because it's permanent.

I've heard of several wealthy people who refuse to leave their entire fortunes to their children because they don't want things to be too easy for them. They aren't being mean or stingy. They just recognize the value inherent in the *process* that got them to where they are today, and they are concerned that if they give unfathomable riches to their children, they might short-circuit the process of growth their kids need to thrive.

Warren Buffett, for example, said he will leave his children "enough money so that they would feel they could do anything, but not so much that they could do nothing."[1] Bill Gates is said to be leaving $10 million for each of his three children. While you and I would probably love to have that much money handed to us, it's not that much compared to the tens of billions the parents are worth. He said about his children, "In terms of their income, they will have to pick a job they like and go to work."[2]

Similarly, God doesn't just hand us every blessing we ask for—immediately and with no participation on our part—because ultimately it would destroy us. Remember, his value system is different from ours. We usually want things as quickly and easily as possible because we value external results such as money, possessions, and comfort. God doesn't mind when things take longer and require more effort because he values internal results: things such as character transformation, wisdom, inner peace, integrity, and love.

If you want not only to survive hard work, but also to receive the blessing that it brings, you need to adjust your value system so it aligns with God's values. Rather than resenting the difficulty of the work we do, you should recognize that it is helping you in both the short term and the long term.

Not long ago, my son started playing basketball. When I dropped him off at practice, I told him, "Other kids might be more skilled, they might have more experience, or they might be able to run faster, but no one should outwork you." Will my son want to play competitive basketball in the years to come? I have no idea, and I'm fine if he doesn't. But I want him to learn that whatever he does, he should do it with all his heart and strength.

I used to run a basketball program in North Carolina. We worked with hundreds, if not thousands, of athletes over the years. Over 150 of our players went on to play college ball, and several of them made it to the NBA. I noticed that many of the players were there because they were naturally gifted, and many others were there because they were incredibly hard workers. But the best players were the ones who had both natural skill *and* a solid work ethic. They didn't just rely on their skill but instead worked hard to improve, contribute to their team, and achieve more than the bare minimum.

Hard work will get you into positions and take you places that ability alone cannot. While it's tempting to rely on skill, luck, connections, cheating, or any other "shortcut," you aren't doing yourself any favors by skipping the hard parts. They are making you the person you need to become.

There will be times in life when you find yourself eastbound on the south side of a mule, and you're going to go through some stuff, face some stuff, and maybe even smell some stuff. Keep plowing, though. Keep your eyes on the goal ahead, and eventually your hard work will pay off.

Hard Work: Questions for Reflection

1. How has your work ethic been shaped by past experiences? Can you identify moments in your life where hard, unpleasant work led to positive outcomes?
2. Have you ever taken a shortcut that ended up slowing you down or leading to unintended consequences? How did that experience shape your approach to work or decision-making?
3. In what areas of your life are you practicing diligence that might not be recognized by others? How do you stay motivated to continue when the rewards are not immediately visible?

Getting Better Through Bumps

Write down a specific area of "hard work" you've been avoiding or resenting. What are the consequences of not addressing this issue? What are the benefits of addressing it? What practical step will you take *today* to embrace hard work?

CONCLUSION

YOU'VE GOT THIS

A friend of mine told me that when he was a little boy and his family would go on road trips, his dad would say, "Hold on to your dentures" every time they were about to hit a big bump in the road. Everyone would then grab onto the little handles above the car windows. My friend naturally concluded those handles were called "dentures," and it was years before he discovered the truth.

On the bumpy road to better, you need to "hold on to your dentures" because some of the bumps are going to send you flying. This means you will also need some handles to hold on to. There will be unexpected events, difficult people, weird comments, confusing seasons, painful realizations, and many, many more hard things to navigate. We've explored twenty-two of them in this book, but there are others.

So what handles should you grab ahold of when you hit bumps along the way? Let me give you four of the most important.

1. Hold on to Jesus.

He's the driver, not you. He knows the road ahead. Even when things are terrifying or traumatic, he's not going to abandon you. Let the bumps point you toward him. At the end of the day, nothing matters more than your relationship with him. Even if you were to lose your money, your health, your friendships, or your reputation, you still have him.

2. Hold on to love.

Love is your compass. It helps you chart a course even when you can't see what's coming. Bumps have a way of shaking everything, but love is stronger than any force, and it will keep you oriented and stable. Love other people, especially those close to you. Hard times remind you of the importance of family and friends, so let the bumps bring you closer to other people.

3. Hold on to curiosity.

What's a road trip without some wonder and awe along the way? So much of life comes down to learning. Rather than expecting to get everything right the first time, expect to learn a lot, to see new things, and to grow. Have an adventurous, courageous, curious spirit. When I was younger, I valued answers; but the older I get, the more I value questions. They keep you open, young, excited, and humble.

4. Hold on to your sense of humor.

Finally, don't take yourself too seriously. Laugh more and stress less. You're not going to get to the end of your life and wish you'd panicked more often or freaked out at more things. You're going to wish you had enjoyed the journey. You're going to wonder why you let fear steal from you. If you can find joy in anything, you'll be unstoppable—and you'll be a lot more fun to be around.

If you're going over some bumps right now, turn to Jesus, keep love at the center, stay curious, and laugh whenever you can. I promise you'll get through this. Not only that, you'll come out stronger than ever. Your resilience is growing with each battle, with each right choice, and with each win. Someday you're going to look back on the season you're in today, and you're going to be glad you pushed through.

You've got this. I believe that with all my heart. You have the grace you need, as well as the wisdom, grit, and resources. You are smart and talented. You have friends and family who care about you. You have a divine call on your life. And most of all, you have Jesus on your side.

Sure, the road is bumpy. But it's the bumpy road *to better*. You're going to love where it takes you and who it makes you.

ACKNOWLEDGMENTS

Jen—there's no road I'd rather walk than the one I'm on with you. Your love, strength, and unwavering belief in me have carried me through every high and low. You are my rock, my greatest gift, and the reason better is always within reach. I love you more than words can say—thank you for everything.

Max—my greatest joy and my greatest motivation. Watching you grow, dream, and become the incredible person you are is one of my life's greatest honors. You inspire me to be better, to keep going, and to never stop believing in what's possible. I love you more than words can express, and I'm so proud to be your dad.

Alexander Field—none of this would be possible without you. Your belief in me, your wisdom, and your steady guidance have shaped this journey in more ways than I can count. I'm forever grateful.

Pastor Dino and DeLynn Rizzo—there aren't enough words to express what you both mean to me. Your love, leadership, and unwavering support have changed my life. I carry your wisdom with me every step of the way. Love you both deeply!

Justin Jaquith—you've been more than a friend; you're a brother. Your attention to detail, encouragement, and unwavering belief in me have made such a difference. Thank you for walking this road with me.

To all my uncles and aunties—your love, wisdom, and prayers have shaped me more than you'll ever know. Thank you for being my foundation, my safe place, and my greatest cheerleaders.

To my friends—you know who you are! This is just the beginning. More laughs, more adventures, more memories—we're in this for life.

And last, but never least—*my family*.

To my mom, Brenda Timberlake—everything I am, I owe to you. Your love is the kind that shapes souls, your wisdom is the kind that builds legacies, and your faith is the kind that moves mountains. Thank you for loving me the way you do.

To my late father, Mack Timberlake Jr.—I pray I'm making you proud. Your voice, your lessons, and your legacy live in me every day. I carry you with me in all that I do.

Tmac and Momma MC—your love for me is undeniable. Thank you for always making me feel that way!

Darrell, Nica, Dayana, Daila, Tim, Chris, Christianson, Carrigan, Quis, George, Majesty, Micah, TT, Kimmy, Scott, and Stevie girl—you make life sweeter. Your love, your laughter, and your presence mean everything. I wouldn't trade this family for the world. Because of you, I am the richest man in the world.

NOTES

Introduction
1. "Tardigrade," *National Geographic*, accessed September 2, 2024, https://www.nationalgeographic.com/animals/invertebrates/facts/tardigrades-water-bears.

Chapter 3
1. Jim Collins, *Good to Great: Why Some Companies Make the Leap . . . and Others Don't* (Harper Business, 2001), 1.

Chapter 4
1. "Newton's Laws of Motion," NASA Glenn Research Center, updated June 27, 2024, https://www1.grc.nasa.gov/beginners-guide-to-aeronautics/newtons-laws-of-motion/.

Chapter 6
1. Robert Longley, "The Great Compromise of 1787," ThoughtCo, updated August 27, 2024, https://www.thoughtco.com/great-compromise-of-1787-3322289.
2. "Compromise," *Oxford Languages* (Oxford University Press, 2025).

Chapter 7
1. Truth and Reconciliation Commission, accessed January 15, 2025, https://www.justice.gov.za/trc/.

Chapter 8

1. Georg Kell, "From Emissions Cheater to Climate Leader: VW's Journey from Dieselgate to Embracing E-Mobility," *Forbes*, December 5, 2022, https://www.forbes.com/sites/georgkell/2022/12/05/from-emissions-cheater-to-climate-leader-vws-journey-from-dieselgate-to-embracing-e-mobility/.
2. "Quote Origin: We Learn from History That We Do Not Learn from History," Quote Investigator, March 6, 2024, https://quoteinvestigator.com/2024/03/06/learn-history/.

Chapter 9

1. Nathaniel Meyersohn, "3 Times Howard Schultz Saved Starbucks," CNN Business, June 5, 2018, https://money.cnn.com/2018/06/05/news/companies/starbucks-howard-schultz-coffee/index.html.
2. Adi Ignatius, "The HBR Interview: 'We Had to Own the Mistakes,'" *Harvard Business Review*, July-August 2010, https://hbr.org/2010/07/the-hbr-interview-we-had-to-own-the-mistakes.

Chapter 10

1. "Peanut Gallery," *Cambridge Dictionary*, https://dictionary.cambridge.org/dictionary/english/peanut-gallery.

Chapter 14

1. "Biggest Comeback in Jaguars History vs. Chargers to Stay Alive," Sounds of the Game, online video, jaguars.com, accessed January 16, 2025, https://www.jaguars.com/video/biggest-comeback-in-jaguars-history-vs-chargers-to-stay-alive-sounds-of-the-game.
2. J. P. Louw and E. A. Nida, *Greek-English Lexicon of the New Testament: Based on Semantic Domains*, electronic ed. of the 2nd ed., vol. 1 (United Bible Societies, 1996), 307.

Chapter 16

1. Drs. Derek and Laura Cabrera, "Relationships Sponsored by the Number 3," *The Cabrera Lab Podcast*, July 24, 2024, https://open

.spotify.com/episode/48VP7LIlDuftkViZj9f9ss?si
=a529d98ebcbe4c24.

Chapter 17

1. Ursula K. Le Guin, *The Language of the Night: Essays on Fantasy and Science Fiction* (Putnam, 1979), 139.
2. *Egypt Today* staff, "et Quote: Naguib Mahfouz," *Egypt Today*, December 11, 2017, https://www.egypttoday.com/Article/6/36367/et-Quote-Naguib-Mahfouz.

Chapter 19

1. Tish Wrigley, "Aung San Suu Kyi," *AnOther Magazine*, April 18, 2012, https://www.anothermag.com/art-photography/1907/aung-san-suu-kyi.
2. Elisabeth Elliot, *Through Gates of Splendor* (Tyndale, 1981), 172.

Chapter 20

1. First written about by Elisabeth Kübler-Ross, *On Death and Dying* (Routledge, 1969).

Chapter 21

1. Michael Ekow Manuel, *Maritime Risk and Organizational Learning* (Ashgate Publishing, 2012), 59.
2. John Maxwell, *The 15 Invaluable Laws of Growth* (Hachette Book Group, 2022), 54.

Chapter 22

1. Carol Loomis, *Tap Dancing to Work: Warren Buffett on Practically Everything, 1966–2012* (Penguin Publishing Group, 2013), 318.
2. Robert Frank, "Bill Gates' Children Mock Him with 'Billionaire' Song," *Wall Street Journal*, June 14, 2011, https://www.wsj.com/articles/BL-WHB-4788.

ABOUT THE AUTHOR

Tim Timberlake serves as the senior pastor of Celebration Church. He's a graduate of the Pistis School of Ministry in Detroit, Michigan. Pastor Tim is a gifted communicator and teacher who has the ability to communicate to people from all walks of life. His sense of humor, combined with his in-depth Bible teaching, give the listener and reader the tools to transform their lives from the inside out. He takes pleasure in the small things, is an avid sports fan, and is a popular thought leader.

Pastor Tim lives in Jacksonville, Florida, with his wife, Jen, and son, Maxwell. The Timberlakes feel most alive when they are pouring back into others, and they seek to glorify God through their lives and family.